Resilient Co-Parenting With a Narcissist

Outsmart Chaos With Effective Boundaries and Communication, Raise Resilient Children With Family-Focused Strategies, and Rediscover Your True Self

Di Stock, BCouns

© **Copyright 2024 - All rights reserved.**

The content contained within this book may not be reproduced, duplicated or transmitted without direct written permission from the author or the publisher.

Under no circumstances will any blame or legal responsibility be held against the publisher, or author, for any damages, reparation, or monetary loss due to the information contained within this book, either directly or indirectly.

Legal Notice:

This book is copyright protected. It is only for personal use. You cannot amend, distribute, sell, use, quote or paraphrase any part, or the content within this book, without the consent of the author or publisher.

Disclaimer Notice:

Please note the information contained within this document is for educational and entertainment purposes only. All effort has been executed to present accurate, up to date, reliable, complete information. No warranties of any kind are declared or implied. Readers acknowledge that the author is not engaged in the rendering of legal, financial, medical or professional advice. The content within this book has been derived from various sources. Please consult a licensed professional before attempting any techniques outlined in this book.

By reading this document, the reader agrees that under no circumstances is the author responsible for any losses, direct or indirect, that are incurred as a result of the use of the information contained within this document, including, but not limited to, errors, omissions, or inaccuracies.

Table of Contents

INTRODUCTION 1

PART 1: PREPARING FOR THE JOURNEY 5

   CHAPTER 1: RESILIENT CO-PARENTING AND NARCISSISM 7
      The Power of Resilient Co-Parenting 7
      The Spectrum of Narcissistic Behavior 8
      The Narcissistic Relationship Cycle 10
      Recognizing Narcissistic Abuse 13
      Self-Assessment Activity 17
   CHAPTER 2: ASSESSING YOUR SITUATION AND GETTING STARTED 21
      What to Consider When Co-Parenting With a Narcissist 21
      Building Your Emotional Resilience 26
      Activity for Overcoming Obstacles on Your Journey 29

PART 2: NAVIGATING CO-PARENTING 31

   CHAPTER 3: SETTING BOUNDARIES AND COMMUNICATING EFFECTIVELY 33
      Understanding Boundaries 33
      Cultivating Effective Boundaries 35
      Practicing Effective Communication 38
      Action Steps 44
   CHAPTER 4: MANAGING CONFLICT 47
      High-Conflict Traits in Narcissists 47
      Conflict Management Strategies 49
      Protecting Your Mental Health 52
      Action Steps 55
   CHAPTER 5: ADDRESSING PARENTAL ALIENATION 57
      Identifying Parental Alienation 57
      Strategies for Countering Alienation 61
      Putting It Into Practice 64
   CHAPTER 6: LEGAL AND FINANCIAL PLANNING 67
      Traversing the Legal System 67
      Financial Planning Before, During, and After Divorce 71
      Practicing Grounding 73

PART 3: FAMILY-FOCUSED STRATEGIES 75

   CHAPTER 7: FOSTERING EMOTIONAL SAFETY AND CREATING A POSITIVE HOME ENVIRONMENT
   77

The Value of Establishing Routines 77
Building a Nurturing and Supportive Atmosphere 79
Action Steps 84

CHAPTER 8: UNDERSTANDING YOUR CHILD'S NEEDS 87
Co-Parenting During Developmental Stages 87
Emotional Indicators of Distress 94
Creating a Safe Home Environment 96
Journaling for Children 98

CHAPTER 9: TRANSITIONING YOUR CHILD BETWEEN HOMES 101
Navigating Transitions 101
Maintaining Discipline Across Households 105
Action Steps 107

CHAPTER 10: HELPING YOUR CHILD BUILD RESILIENCE 109
Helping Your Child Cope With Separation and Divorce 109
Encouraging Emotional Expression 111
Building Self-Esteem and Confidence 114

PART 4: HEALING AND PERSONAL GROWTH 117

CHAPTER 11: LEARNING TO PRIORITIZE YOURSELF 119
Understanding Your Past to Build a Better Future 119
To Get Different, We Must Do Different 121
Moving Forward 127
Self-Reflection Journaling Challenge 129

CHAPTER 12: REDISCOVERING YOURSELF 131
Finding Yourself After Divorce 131
Embrace New Opportunities in Your Life 134
Rediscovery Bucket List 135

CONCLUSION 139

APPENDIX A: LEGAL AND FINANCIAL RESOURCES 143

RESOURCES SUPPORT GROUPS 143
LEGAL RESOURCES 143
Legal Aid Resources 144
Parenting Plan Information 144
Custody Arrangement Resources 145
Budgeting Templates 145
FINANCIAL RESOURCES 145

REFERENCES 147

IMAGE REFERENCES 165

Introduction

Rise above the noise, stay resilient, and let your actions speak louder than their chaos. –Di Stock

The decision to separate from or divorce a partner—especially one with whom you chose to have children—is not a decision you make lightly. But when your ex-partner's narcissistic tendencies leave you feeling worn down, anxious, and overwhelmed, you have to do what's best for you and your child. Take a moment to acknowledge that making it this far is proof that you're stronger than you think.

Leaving a toxic relationship while embarking on the co-parenting journey will have its fair share of challenges. After all, you're working to heal from your relationship and the hurt your ex-partner has inflicted while working toward being a good parent and role model for your child.

But if your ex-partner ever made you feel guilty about focusing on yourself, taking time to rest and care for your well-being can be challenging—you may even feel guilty. However, the effort you put in benefits your mental and emotional well-being as well as your ability to show up for your child. You're not being selfish, you're recognizing your worth and showing yourself the respect you have always deserved.

The key to succeeding is developing your resilience. Resilience allows you to overcome the obstacles you encounter on your healing and parenting journey in a way that benefits your overall well-being. It also allows you to grow as a person so that you emerge with new skills and knowledge. That's why this book will utilize resilience as the main tool for your and your child's healing journey.

My work as a counselor has allowed me to support and guide couples, children, and families as they go through some of life's most challenging moments—including co-parenting with a narcissist. I understand the difficulties and emotional turmoil that arise during this journey. My goal is to give you the tools and information you need to build your resilience as a parent and individual so that you can begin healing from your relationship with your ex-partner. But first, what is narcissism?

Narcissism goes beyond simple selfishness. It exists on a spectrum and encompasses traits that can be exhibited to varying degrees, often causing harm to others. Your reasons for leaving your ex-partner likely include the impact that traits such as a constant need for admiration, a strong sense of entitlement, consistent lack of empathy, arrogance, manipulative behavior (like gaslighting and emotional blackmail), and the belief that they're special and unique had on you and your child. These are also the key traits of narcissism.

Being in a relationship with someone who exhibits these characteristics—even to a minor degree—can make maintaining the relationship and creating a positive environment for your child very challenging. Leaving the toxic relationship and environment may be your best course of action. However, separation and divorce also mean keeping your child's best interests in mind, potentially preventing you from completely cutting your ex-partner out of your life. This is where resilient co-parenting comes in.

Co-parenting allows you to fulfill your parental responsibilities alongside your ex-partner while ensuring your child's needs and best interests remain the main goals. This parenting strategy can be extremely beneficial for children and lead to a lower risk of behavioral issues after divorce. But your ex-partner's narcissistic behaviors can create additional challenges.

However, you may have to choose a different parenting style depending on the severity of your ex-partner's narcissistic traits, if they are emotionally or physically abusive, and their regular treatment of you and your child.

Parallel parenting is a great second option. It allows divorced parents with high-conflict relationships to fulfill their parenting responsibilities and ensure their child's needs are put first without either parent having to interact. Any interactions that occur are minimal and often determined and guided by a set of legally enforceable rules. This ensures all parties remain protected.

In cases where your ex-partner poses an immediate danger to the health and safety of your child, you should also pursue legal action to prevent them from having contact with your child. Remember that narcissism prevents your ex-partner from moving past their ego and putting your child and their needs first—regardless of their age—making it difficult for them to fulfill their parenting responsibilities properly.

The main goal of this book is to help you achieve a balance between taking care of yourself and your needs, while also meeting your child's needs during co-parenting. The strategies and tools provided throughout this book will help you rebuild your life and create a healthier and more positive home environment for you and your child. It will also guide you on your parenting and healing journey regardless of the parenting style you choose.

We'll start by looking at the impact of your ex-partner's narcissistic tendencies on you and your family, as well as their impact on the co-parenting dynamic. This creates the foundation for you to successfully use the tools and strategies for achieving co-parenting success without sacrificing your or your child's mental and emotional well-being.

Learning to enforce boundaries and communicate effectively are two crucial tools for success. They're great for navigating life and can benefit your child's relationship with your ex-partner when you aren't around. This also prepares your child to deal with challenging people throughout their lives.

Problems like parental alienation will also be discussed so that you can prevent your ex-partner from ruining your relationship with your child or hurting them. This helps you create a safe and positive home environment where your child can thrive, too.

Co-parenting with an ex-partner who has narcissistic tendencies is possible. No matter your current situation or the life you have led up until now, you can create a healthier and happier life for yourself and your child. And even if the steps you take are small, they will help you reach your goals as a parent and individual. So, take back control over your life right now and turn the page.

Part 1:

Preparing for the Journey

Prepare with purpose and walk this path with resilience. The first step in resilient co-parenting with a narcissist is believing in your own strength and the brighter days ahead. –Di Stock

Chapter 1:
Resilient Co-Parenting and Narcissism

When co-parenting with a narcissist, resilience isn't optional—it's your superpower.
–Di Stock

Resilience is the key to success when co-parenting with a narcissist. The methods you use to develop this crucial trait also aid your healing journey. Before we dive into how you can nurture your resilience and navigate co-parenting with your ex-partner, we first have to understand the relationship between co-parenting and resilience.

The Power of Resilient Co-Parenting

Being resilient means having the skills and tools needed to cope with life's challenges in a way that protects your overall well-being and gives you room to grow as a person. Parenting alongside a person with narcissistic traits is difficult. However, developing your resilience can protect you from further harm caused by your ex-partner. It also becomes easier to focus on your child's needs while caring for yourself. Three main habits define a resilient individual's ability to navigate adversity and recover from challenging situations:

- **They accept reality:** You have to recognize that challenging situations are inevitable. Accepting that they happen allows you to face them without feeling like you've been unfairly targeted. This means accepting that your ex-partner may not change and, instead, navigating their narcissistic behaviors to protect yourself and your child when co-parenting.

- **Focus on what can be changed:** When faced with a challenge, identify what you can change in that moment. This empowers you to take back control. While you can't change your ex-partner's behavior, for example, you can still acknowledge and appreciate the good in your life.

- **Choosing a helpful response:** Negative thoughts aren't helpful, so it's better to focus on the thoughts and actions that can help improve the situation. You can then choose a response that benefits you and your child. We'll practice this skill in the next chapter.

These habits provide insight into the obstacles you may face on your journey. Such insight is valuable for effectively implementing the strategies needed to overcome them.

For example, your ex-partner could try to convince you that your child would like a specific change in the parenting plan, while you know your ex-partner is trying to manipulate you into making a choice that benefits them and inconveniences you and your child.

Accepting that you aren't responsible for your ex-partner's behavior allows you to take a deep breath and acknowledge that their behavior is frustrating. Instead of reacting or arguing, you'll use skills like active listening and your parenting plan to help you respond appropriately. It also reminds you to ask for help from your legal representative, if needed. This is where understanding what narcissism is can be helpful.

The Spectrum of Narcissistic Behavior

Narcissistic personality disorder (NPD) is a mental health condition that impacts how a person views themselves and the world around them. It's characterized by an intense and constant need to feel important, leading to behaviors that may be harmful to other people. Behaviors that are erratic, dramatic, irrational, and emotional are also connected to this condition.

A person can display narcissistic traits to varying degrees because this condition exists on a spectrum. A person whose traits fall on the higher end of the spectrum is more likely to be diagnosed with NPD, while a person whose traits fall on the middle to lower end of the spectrum may go about their lives as normal.

However, those closest to them—like spouses, children, and friends—will still be harmed on an emotional, mental, and physical level. This means that a person can exhibit narcissistic traits without having NPD, but their behaviors, words, and actions can still be extremely harmful.

Let's look at the main types of NPDs and how they could manifest in everyday life.

Malignant Narcissism

This category is characterized by a severe sense of superiority, egocentric and self-absorbed behavior, and a sadistic streak. It can manifest in many ways, like your ex-partner controlling who you spend time with; mocking or humiliating you; acting aggressively toward people they believe are criticizing them; dismissing, ignoring, or mocking your emotions and experiences; and using physical and emotional abuse because it pleases them to see you hurt.

Overt Narcissism

Overt narcissists are obsessed with how other people see them and will use flattery to try and gain power. They may fish for compliments and appear popular since their charisma makes others want to spend time with them. However, they lack empathy, are very opinionated, and demand to be constantly praised.

Many overt narcissists gain power and wealth that they share in return for praise, affection, and favors that benefit them. If they believe you're going to leave or have betrayed them (even when you haven't), they'll use their power and wealth to get revenge, like destroying your reputation.

Covert Narcissist

This category is often undetected and subtle, but it's still harmful. Highly sensitive to criticism, covert narcissists act unaffected by using sarcastic remarks or being dismissive. Passive aggression is a common manipulation tactic used to make the narcissist appear superior. The silent treatment, mocking you while pretending they're just joking, sabotaging your work and friendships, and blaming you or someone else when they're at fault are examples of covert narcissism.

Antagonistic Narcissism

Characterized by extreme rivalry, competitiveness, and arrogance, this form of narcissism results in constant and open criticism of others. They may also demand you listen to them and do what they tell you to, belittle you and others, believe they deserve special treatment in every situation, and threaten or use physical violence to get their way.

While narcissism manifests in different ways, the behaviors exhibited by these individuals are intended to cause you and your child physical, mental, and emotional harm. In romantic relationships, these behaviors lead to a specific pattern.

The Narcissistic Relationship Cycle

Individuals with narcissistic tendencies often struggle to maintain interpersonal relationships. Instead, they rely on an abusive pattern of behavior to keep the other person (like their partner, friend, or coworker) in their life, creating a repeating cycle that's extremely harmful to that person.

By understanding this pattern, you can break it and avoid being sucked back in. This is crucial since co-parenting means maintaining some degree of contact with your ex-partner. But remember that your experience with this cycle may differ compared to other individuals. That's because there are many types of narcissistic relationship dynamics.

In the following cycle, we'll use the empath and narcissist dynamic to understand how this pattern could manifest even though it isn't the only pattern that exists.

Idealization Stage

The narcissist will use charm, flattery, gifts, and attention to convince you that you're special and unique. They may also try to move the relationship quickly by acting overwhelmingly attracted to you. The goal is to manipulate you so that you remain in the relationship.

In a relationship with an empath, the narcissist is drawn to the empath's compassionate and nurturing nature. The empath is drawn to the apparent confidence and charm of the narcissist. This makes it challenging for the empath to realize their new partner is a narcissist.

Devaluation Stage

Now that you're firmly attached to the narcissist and committed to the relationship, they will use subtle techniques meant to convince you that you've done something wrong. This includes hints that you've hurt their feelings or forgotten something important using strategies like passive-aggressiveness, name-calling, comparing you to others, subtle criticism, and humiliation.

You may also be accused of things you never did, and the pressure the narcissist applies while doing so will cause you to doubt yourself. This is known as "gaslighting" and can cause your self-esteem and confidence to decrease so that you rely on the narcissist even more.

The kindness of the empath is exploited during this stage, as the narcissist begins implementing emotionally abusive techniques like gaslighting to stay in control.

Repetition Stage

Now that you feel confused, anxious, depressed, and scared over the possible loss of your relationship with the narcissist, you may try to please them; or you may pull away from them to protect yourself. If you pull away, your ex-partner may become angrier.

At this stage, the empath may feel like it's their fault that the narcissist is treating them this way, causing them to attempt to fix the relationship even if it means they're harmed (physically, mentally, or emotionally) in the process.

Discard Stage

There are many ways in which this stage can manifest. Your ex-partner could decide that the relationship is finished and that you no longer matter to them, or you may be the one to realize that your ex-partner is abusing you and leave them.

The empath will recognize the toxic behavior patterns of the narcissist and decide that protecting their mental and emotional health means they have to leave the narcissist.

Hoovering Stage

Think of this stage like a vacuum cleaner that tries to suck you back into your relationship with your ex-partner. Even if you were the one to decide to leave first, your ex-partner may attempt to reignite a relationship with you, causing the cycle to repeat. Love bombing (using gifts and compliments), fake apologies, and false promises may be used to try and suck you back into their life. This is a form of emotional warfare and can be extremely damaging.

In the narcissist and empath dynamic, charm and guilt are used to try and pull the empath back into the relationship soon after the discard stage.

If you can resist the narcissist, firmly remind yourself that they have not changed, and maintain your boundaries, you can escape them. This will be especially important during co-parenting since remaining in contact with your ex-partner can make it challenging to avoid dealing with this stage of the cycle.

Identifying this pattern and remaining vigilant is only the first step to preventing this cycle from repeating during your co-parenting journey. The next section will arm you with further knowledge of the tools your ex-partner will try to use against you.

Recognizing Narcissistic Abuse

When you are a victim of narcissistic abuse, it can be difficult to acknowledge that you've been abused. Many victims of this form of abuse feel overwhelmed by feelings of anxiety, confusion, and self-doubt—emotions that arise due to the tactics their ex-partner has been using to manipulate them and remain in control.

By developing your knowledge of these tactics, you take away some of their power. This makes it easier to resist them, especially when your ex-partner tries to suck you back into the relationship. We'll start with the different red flags your ex-partner may exhibit throughout the co-parenting relationship.

Behavioral Red Flags

During your relationship with your ex-partner, they likely displayed several red flags. They may also exhibit these behaviors throughout your co-parenting relationship. Learning to identify red flags, using the following list, will help you to start taking back control:

- **Controlling behavior:** What you wear, who you spend time with, and how you spend your money may be determined by your ex-partner. They could also insist on making as many decisions as possible for you and your child.

- **Disrespecting boundaries:** Your ex-partner's actions may not align with their words, resulting in your boundaries being crossed. Stalking your social media, tracking your location all the time, and moving the relationship as fast as possible are a few examples.

- **Gaslighting:** Using your words against you, threatening to punish you, and questioning your understanding of a situation and your experiences are gaslighting tactics used to manipulate you.

- **Social isolation:** To prevent their control over you from being disrupted, your ex-partner may isolate you from hobbies, family, friends, and other things you love. This may include limited phone access and no access to your money.

- **Censorship:** To maintain their image and protect their ego, the narcissist may tell you what information you can and cannot share with other people. This could include telling you how to behave when you are out in public.

- **Verbal abuse and threats:** The silent treatment (a form of abuse that occurs by withholding attention), name-calling, yelling, and demeaning behavior are forms of verbal abuse intended to punish you in some way. The narcissist may even threaten self-harm, the people you love, or your pets to control you.

- **Lack of empathy:** This defining trait of narcissism shows that the narcissist doesn't truly care about you. Instead, they will victimize themselves and draw the focus to them, dismissing your emotions or telling you how you are feeling even if it isn't true.

Emotional and Psychological Symptoms

Narcissistic abuse, regardless of how long you have to endure it, can have short- and long-term effects on your emotional and psychological health. Chronic narcissistic abuse may also lead to additional conditions like post-traumatic stress disorder (PTSD). This condition manifests when you've had a traumatic experience, and an emotionally or physically harmful relationship with an individual who has narcissistic tendencies is one example.

Narcissistic victim syndrome (NVS) is another condition caused by long-term narcissistic abuse. This syndrome can trigger a sense of toxic shame, depressive symptoms, increased anxiety, a constant state of hypervigilance, and emotional flashbacks of the abusive incident.

Different people will also have unique experiences even if they experienced similar situations. That doesn't mean your trauma isn't valid. In the following list, you'll find the most common emotional and psychological signs of abuse:

- **Self-isolation:** Seclusion occurs due to a sense of shame about the abuse you've experienced, including a fear that no one will believe you.

- **Dissociation:** This helps you stay safe and block out the intense pain and terror of your circumstances. It can lead to lapses in memory, a loss of your sense of self, emotional numbness, and an altered perception.

- **Self-sabotage:** This is in the form of negative self-talk and destructive habits that result from the feelings of worthlessness your ex-partner forced on you.

- **Difficulty focusing:** You struggle to focus on your basic needs and desires since you've always had to focus on the needs of your ex-partner.

- **Finding it hard to do the things you love:** Doing things you enjoy, such as hobbies, is harder since your ex-partner may have tried to punish you in some way for succeeding or pursuing your goals.

- **Trust issues:** You have challenges trusting others even after the relationship has ended because of the way you were treated by a person who was supposed to love and cherish you. It can also become difficult to trust yourself and your decisions.

- **Being cautious:** You may constantly feel like you have to remain cautious and on edge to prevent further harm even when you are in a safe environment with people you can trust.

- **Rationalizing the abuse:** Rationalizing what you experienced or denying it occurs due to the manipulation you endured from the narcissist. Instead, you internalize your fear and blame yourself even though the abuse you've endured is not, and never will be, your fault.

- **Anxiety and depression:** When you've had to endure abuse of any kind, the constant feelings of anxiety and depression you experience can make it challenging to find hope. This contributes to an increased risk of self-harm and, possibly, suicide as a way to cope.

From the above list, we can see that the impact of the abuse you've experienced is serious. But how do these effects manifest?

- Low levels of self-esteem result from constant criticism, manipulation, and belittlement from the abuser.

- Poor mental health may result in PTSD, NVS, anxiety, depression, outbursts of anger, difficulty regulating your emotions, and emotional numbness.

- You may experience obstacles in future relationships, such as difficulty trusting your partner.

- Physical health problems like poor sleep quality, stomach issues, headaches, and muscle tension can arise due to neglecting your own needs or the adoption of unhealthy habits to cope with the abuse.

Healing from the emotional and psychological effects of narcissistic abuse includes setting boundaries, forgiving yourself, being patient with yourself as you heal, building a support network of parents in similar situations, asking for help from a professional, and taking better care of yourself.

These are also strategies that will help you become a resilient co-parent and redefine your relationship with your ex-partner. But how can we put the information from this chapter into action?

Self-Assessment Activity

By turning your thoughts into a physical form, you can reflect on them, make connections, and better understand what's happening inside your mind and heart. In a journal or notebook, answer the following questions to aid your understanding of how your ex-partner has treated you:

1. Did your ex-partner frequently dismiss or ignore your emotions?

2. Does your ex-partner blame other people for their actions or words?

3. Have you ever noticed your ex-partner manipulating a situation so that they would benefit?

4. Does your ex-partner frequently put their needs first?

5. Is it common for your ex-partner to guilt you when you spend time with other people or on your hobbies?

6. Do they tend to show little to no empathy for other people?

7. When you express your needs or boundaries, does your ex-partner get angry or try to dismiss you?

8. Has your ex-partner ever mocked your abilities, character, or accomplishments?

9. Do they frequently ignore or dismiss your feelings, thoughts, or opinions?

10. Are your feelings, thoughts, or experiences frequently and consistently denied or criticized by your ex-partner?

11. Have you ever felt as though your ex-partner is pressuring you in any way, even when they don't directly threaten you?

12. Use the red flags from this chapter to identify the red flags in your relationship with your ex-partner.

13. Reflect on the early days of your relationship and write down at least three instances during which you felt uncomfortable and explain why.

14. List the ways your ex-partner manipulated you. Add to this list when you remember something new as it will help you notice this behavior during the co-parenting journey.

15. What behaviors will you never tolerate again now that you've separated from your ex-partner?

Your answers to this self-assessment will form the foundation needed to help figure out what behaviors you will and won't tolerate in your co-parenting relationship. So, keep this activity on hand as you work through future chapters.

Developing resilience and healing from your relationship with your ex-partner also has many benefits for your mental and emotional health. So, how do you balance co-parenting with healing? Turn the page to find out.

Chapter 2:

Assessing Your Situation and Getting Started

Assess your reality and recognize your challenges. Getting started means understanding where you stand. –Di Stock

Since your co-parenting situation will be unique to you and the relationship you have with your ex-partner, you need tools that will help you make informed decisions that take your ex-partner's narcissistic tendencies into account. The previous chapter will have helped you better understand your relationship with your ex-partner and what narcissistic behaviors you will no longer tolerate. Now it's time to consider how you can fulfill your rights and responsibilities to your child in a way that builds your resilience too.

What to Consider When Co-Parenting With a Narcissist

Co-parenting with your ex-partner can seem impossible because of their narcissistic tendencies. There are situations where this is true, such as when your ex-partner poses an immediate danger to you and your child's continued health and safety. With resilient co-parenting, you can use various tools like effective communication strategies, boundary setting, organization of parental responsibilities, a legal parenting plan, persistence, and consistency to make this possible.

A parenting plan will be a valuable tool when co-parenting with a narcissist. This plan is a type of legal contract between you and your ex-partner that states exactly what will be expected from each parent. This ensures your ex-partner will be held legally liable for any narcissistic and abusive behaviors that lead to the breaking of this contract. We will take a closer look at how to use a parenting plan in Chapter 6.

Keep in mind that separating from your ex-partner doesn't mean they won't exhibit narcissistic tendencies. You and your child will still be at risk of emotional abuse and toxic behavior as a result of your ex-partner's inability to see past their own needs and ego. They may also make it impossible for you, family members, legal representatives, and counselors to provide them with helpful feedback and parenting suggestions.

If your ex-partner's narcissistic tendencies are severe, leading to a tumultuous co-parenting relationship, then you may need to opt for parallel parenting. This parenting style—which also allows for legal protections to be used—allows each parent to fulfill their parental rights and responsibilities and maintain a good relationship with their child. It also limits the contact you have with your ex-partner, resulting in fewer occasions for conflict that hurts you and your child.

Divorcing and separating from your ex-partner may also have ripple effects on your extended family. The goal is to keep your child's best interests at the forefront and extended family can provide your child with additional love, guidance, and support throughout your child's life. This can be crucial during the period of instability that often arises during divorce due to the changes occurring.

While extended family may not be your child's parents, they should still be a part of your child's life. It's important that you communicate honestly with them about the co-parenting arrangement and rules too. This helps your child's aunts, uncles, grandparents, and close family friends better understand what will be expected of them now that you and your ex-partner have separated and the family dynamic has changed.

If your child's relationship with your ex-partner's family is healthy and safe, they should be encouraged to maintain a relationship with your child. However, if there are concerns about your child's safety and well-being, you may need to acquire legal guidance from a family lawyer who can mediate disputes and help you ensure that your child's safety, needs, and well-being remain the top priority.

Tips for Getting Started

We'll discuss the strategies needed to effectively co-parent with your ex-partner in later chapters, but you can use the following tips to help you get started:

- Don't waste your energy on trying to change your ex-partner.

- Pursue legal protection for you and your child in the form of a parenting plan to prevent and limit your ex-partner's opportunities to manipulate or control you and your child.

- Remember that you don't have to be a perfect parent, but you can do your best to protect your child from your ex-partner, and that will be more important.

- Take time to listen to input from your extended family and consider whether their suggestions could help you on your co-parenting journey.

- Consider seeking help from a therapist, mediator, or counselor who can help you care for your mental and emotional well-being, and interact with your ex-partner while staying calm.

These are just a few helpful tips to give you a better idea of what co-parenting with your ex-partner might look like. Now it's time to dive into what may be expected of you during the co-parenting journey.

What Are Your Parental Rights and Responsibilities?

If you're divorced, in the process of divorce, or separated, you will need to remember that you and your ex-partner will still have legal rights and responsibilities as parents that you need to fulfill. While the legal process can be daunting, understanding your rights and responsibilities, as well as navigating the family court system successfully, can help you build a healthier and happier life with your child away from your ex-partner without violating any laws. So, what's the role of family court?

This specialized court was created for legal matters relating to children and family relationships. Activities relating to guardianship, family offenses, paternity, and child neglect are a few examples of the activities this court takes care of. And while they don't handle divorce, custody cases are often referred to this court.

However, every country and state will have slightly different laws and procedures regarding custody and parental rights. Be sure to do your own research on your country's and state's laws, as well as your local family court, to ensure that you have the right information. This is especially vital if your ex-partner's narcissistic behaviors make it unsafe for your child to spend time with them, and you have to pursue legal assistance. A lawyer can help you navigate this court effectively and keep your child safe, so consider seeking their guidance.

This is also when custody comes into play. This term encompasses the legal authority that you as a parent have to care for your child and make decisions about their life and well-being, including factors such as education and religious upbringing. Take note that the phrase "parental rights and responsibilities" is often used interchangeably with the term "custody" but they mean the same thing.

The type of custody arrangement will depend on several factors, including your and your ex-partner's individual ability to protect your child and meet their needs. Custody arrangements are often made during the divorce process, so you may already be familiar with them. If you're still in the process of separating from your ex-partner, it would be best to consult your lawyer to understand your options and what will be expected of you. In Chapter 6 and Appendix A, you will find additional legal resources that you can use to understand these arrangements better and seek help.

If you have been assigned as the "custodial parent," it means that you will have more parental rights and responsibilities compared to your ex-partner, who will be labeled the "noncustodial parent." Keep in mind that these terms and their meanings can differ depending on the country you live in, so be sure to speak with your lawyer and do your research. The court will be responsible for determining the type of custody assigned to each parent, so what could custody look like in this example?

As the custodial parent, your child will spend the majority of their time with you. You will be responsible for fulfilling their basic needs, taking them to and from school and after-school activities, and acting as the main parent. Your ex-partner, on the other hand, may only see your child every second weekend and have fewer parental responsibilities.

However, if the court decides that your ex-partner poses a danger to your child, they may either terminate their parental rights, issue a protection order, or allow supervised access. Again, this will differ depending on your country and state's laws. This occurs in cases where physical, mental, and emotional abuse has been proven to the court. So your ex-partner will no longer be considered the legal parent of your child. This decision is not made lightly, and the court will make its choice by evaluating your unique situation and considering the laws of the state you live in.

In addition to parental rights, you also have specific responsibilities to your child. These are the duties that you and your ex-partner will be required to fulfill when your child is in your care. In the list below, you'll find the most important responsibilities that you will need to fulfill:

- Protect your child from emotional, mental, and physical abuse, as well as other potential threats to their safety.

- Provide a safe and positive living environment.

- Food, shelter, and water should all be provided to your child without expecting anything in return.

- Invest in your child's education by ensuring they go to school and helping them with their schoolwork.

- Take time to get to know your child and understand their interests.

The parenting plan will likely set out the specific rights and responsibilities that you and your ex-partner will need to fulfill. For example, it could help each parent track child-related expenses, the activities each parent is responsible for taking their child to (like sports clubs and doctor's appointments), and the dates and times your child will spend with each parent.

So, while co-parenting allows you and your ex-partner to parent your child separately to some degree, you will both still have specific rights and responsibilities to fulfill. As this can be challenging due to your ex-partner's narcissistic tendencies, you must continue to develop your resilience.

Building Your Emotional Resilience

Building emotional resilience is one method that helps you prioritize your mental health, cope with the challenges you encounter due to your ex-partner's narcissistic tendencies, and focus on your child.

The previous chapter explained why resilience is so important when co-parenting with a narcissist. This trait helps you face life's challenges head-on, acknowledge that they're temporary, and use healthy coping mechanisms to help you overcome them, allowing you to emerge stronger and adapt to the changes that the obstacle may have created.

You do this by learning to express your emotions healthily, accepting yourself as you are, showing yourself forgiveness and patience, building your self-esteem, responding to stress in a way that doesn't hurt you or your child, and learning how to stay in the present by practicing mindfulness. But how do you start building on the habits of resilience from the previous chapter?

Combating Negative Thoughts

After the hurt and trauma you've experienced, negative thoughts may appear, but that doesn't mean they're true. What matters is your willingness to evaluate the thought and move on in a way that benefits you.

In your journal, create two columns and label the first column "List A" and the second one "List B." Then follow the steps below:

1. In List A, write down any negative thoughts you frequently experience (or write them down as they appear).

2. Pick one negative thought and look at it without asking why you thought that.

3. In List B, rewrite the negative thought so that it's realistic and positive.

For example, I could put the following thought in List A, "I'm afraid that my ex-partner was right, and I won't be a good parent." We know that the narcissistic tendencies of the ex-partner mean that they were likely trying to manipulate and control us by telling us we're incapable of being a good parent without them.

When I rephrase this thought in List B, it may look like, "I might make mistakes and need to ask for help from people I trust, but I will still do my best to be a good parent because my child doesn't need me to be perfect, they just need me to be there."

When comparing the two thoughts, the thought in List B reminds us that we're human and that it's okay to make mistakes and ask for help. That doesn't make us any less worthy or our child any less loved.

This activity can also be helpful to practice with your child. It teaches them that while they might have negative thoughts (which may also have been triggered by your ex-partner), it doesn't mean those thoughts are true. It also helps them reshape these thoughts into ones that help them believe in their capabilities and self-worth, boosting their confidence.

Another valuable way to help you develop your resilience is to connect with people who are going through similar situations, are parents themselves, or who can simply offer you support when you need someone to talk to.

Building a Support Network

A strong support network can be crucial when you're co-parenting since the members of this system can offer physical and emotional support, help you feel less alone on your journey, encourage you to continue healing, and provide you with friendship and encouragement.

Your ex-partner likely isolated you from the people and things you cared about. This was one of the many methods they may have used to control and manipulate you. The best way to fight back and maintain control over your life when co-parenting is to have a strong support network you can rely on. This community connection can include the parents of your child's friends, parents in the community, parents whose ex-partners also have narcissistic tendencies, your parents, siblings, friends, and counselors you may be seeing.

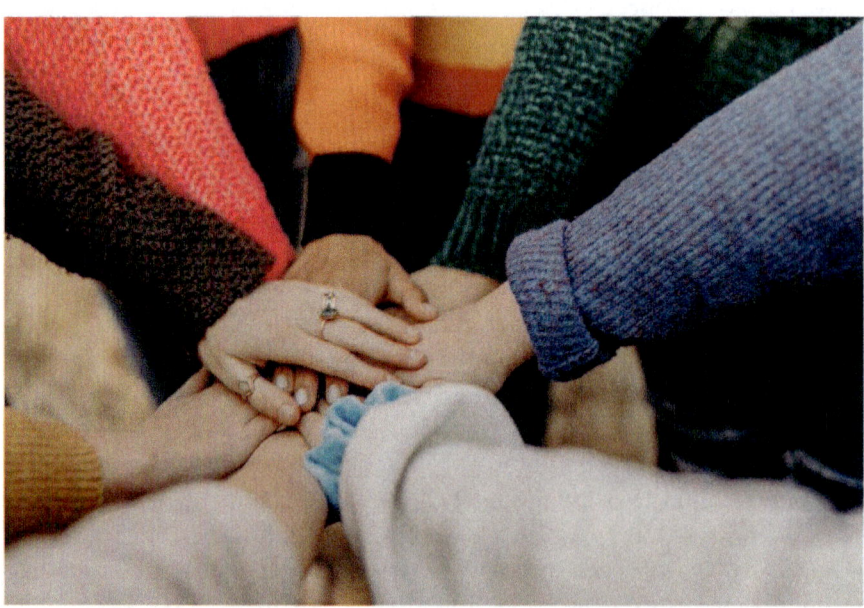

Family and friends are a great starting point for your network. If your relationships with them were damaged, you'll need to start this process by repairing them. Keep in mind that co-parenting and divorce mean that the members of your support network will play slightly different roles while also offering your child additional support, stability, and love. Open and honest communication are a great starting point. You could also speak with a counselor or psychologist for additional assistance, depending on the severity of the damage caused by your ex-partner.

In the following list, you'll find a few tips for seeking help and building your support network:

- Use online resources and community groups. Social media platforms like Facebook are a great way to connect with parents in similar situations.

- Take time to connect with the parents of your child's friends.

- Join societies and volunteering groups aimed at parents.

- Visit your local library or recreation center, as they often have the details of local groups and activities aimed at parents.

- Refer to Appendix A for additional resources to help you find support groups.

Using the tools and strategies from this book, you'll figure out what resilience looks like to you while developing the skills you need to cope with the challenges of co-parenting with a partner who has narcissistic tendencies. And the information from this chapter is only the beginning.

Activity for Overcoming Obstacles on Your Journey

This activity focuses on adjusting how you perceive a challenging situation. While a sudden and unexpected obstacle can fill your mind with negative thoughts, turning the problem upside down helps you find the good in the situation. By reframing your view, you can enter every interaction with your ex-partner with a more positive outlook, regardless of their behavior.

1. In your journal, write down one challenge that you're currently facing.

2. Evaluate the challenge objectively and think about how this obstacle will help you grow and build toward a healthier you.

3. Write down your new view below the obstacle.

You must remain aware of your thoughts and internal voice, and this activity will help you develop this skill. Next, we will look at how you can rebuild and reinforce the boundaries meant to protect your mental, emotional, and physical well-being.

Part 2:

Navigating Co-Parenting

Resilient co-parenting is about creating calm amid the chaos. Stay strong, stay focused, and lead with love. –Di Stock

Chapter 3:
Setting Boundaries and Communicating Effectively

Boundaries protect your peace; communication ensures your voice is heard. Both are nonnegotiables. –Di Stock

Individuals with narcissistic tendencies thrive on the positive and negative reactions of other people. Your ex-partner may purposefully try to cross a boundary because they like to see you get riled up. Or maybe they're unhappy that you're standing your ground and refusing to give them any control over you. As such, boundary setting and effective communication are vital tools for helping you resiliently co-parent with your ex-partner. But this means understanding how to use these tools effectively.

Understanding Boundaries

Boundaries are an effective tool that helps you communicate to others what behaviors toward you are acceptable and unacceptable. However, boundary setting can be challenging when you're co-parenting with a narcissist—especially since your boundaries may have already been repeatedly crossed throughout your relationship with your ex-partner. So, even the smallest success during establishing and maintaining your new boundaries should be recognized and celebrated.

Boundary setting is meant to help your ex-partner understand what is expected of them during the co-parenting journey. Since boundaries can be personal or mutual, they allow you and your ex-partner to put your child's needs first without talking about your thoughts and feelings toward each other or your past relationship.

The boundaries you set will also communicate to your extended family what behaviors toward you and your child will and won't be tolerated, what you expect from them, and how they can respect your personal space.

Standing your ground and maintaining your boundaries—especially when you first set and enforce them—will be crucial to showing your ex-partner, family, and friends that you're serious. Before we look at how to set boundaries, you need to understand the four main boundaries you could set.

Types of Boundaries

In this section, you'll find the four main boundaries you will need to set with your ex-partner to help you resiliently co-parent.

Emotional or Mental Boundaries

You deserve to have your emotions and mental health protected. This boundary establishes emotional safety and protects personal information you don't want to share with your ex-partner or extended family. It could include telling your ex-partner that you aren't available to listen to feelings or concerns that don't involve your child, even if your ex-partner has asked you to.

Remind yourself that you also get to decide what experiences and feelings are shared with other people. You may want to justify your behaviors and decisions to your ex-partner or family members, but they don't need an explanation. Think of it like this: Would they explain those same behaviors or decisions to you?

Additionally, the goal of creating emotional and mental boundaries is to protect yourself against burnout, emotional manipulation, and stress. You can do this by allowing yourself to practice emotional detachment. This technique is valuable for conserving your mental and emotional energy, as well as your time—resources that are precious and shouldn't be wasted on an ex-partner who only wants to control you.

Physical Boundaries

Protecting your privacy and the right not to be touched without your consent can be achieved by establishing physical boundaries. This boundary is helpful if you don't feel comfortable with your ex-partner being in your personal space or hugging you, for example. Additionally, physical boundaries should also be established and practiced at your place of work and at home.

Communication Boundaries

Setting communication boundaries helps you manage when (the time of day) and how (in-person or using text and email) your ex-partner communicates with you and your child. This includes the type of language they use, like not speaking to you respectfully and using insults. It also provides you with an opportunity to document your interactions.

Digital Boundaries

You can decide whether your ex-partner will be allowed to follow or interact with you on social media, including posting pictures of you or talking about you. You can also decide whether you would prefer to only communicate with your ex-partner via digital platforms like email, text, or through applications like Our Family Wizard.

While there are different types of boundaries, they are often set in a very similar manner. So, how do you generate boundaries that are effective against a person with narcissistic tendencies?

Cultivating Effective Boundaries

You may already have boundaries but they may need to be adjusted to ensure they're effective enough to protect you against your ex-partner while co-parenting. Remember that effective boundaries can be the key to achieving the change you seek for yourself and your co-parenting relationship.

While you can set boundaries on your own, it can be helpful to work with a trusted friend or a counselor who can provide positive feedback and help you hold yourself accountable during this process. They could also provide you with the insight you need to succeed.

Start this process by deciding what expectations you have for yourself, your child, your life, your ex-partner, and your extended family. These expectations include behaviors you will and won't tolerate, the type of language used during in-person and written conversations, and how you are treated in general. Chapter 1's self-assessment activity helped lay the groundwork for this step.

Once you understand your expectations, you can create a list of boundaries you'd like to set before following these three steps:

1. Rewrite each boundary in your list so that you directly state your need or request.

2. Refine each boundary so that it's clear and leaves no room to be misinterpreted.

3. Communicate your boundaries clearly to your ex-partner using the communication strategies from the second half of this chapter.

    A. This step can be uncomfortable and trigger shame, guilt, or remorse.

    B. Remind yourself that a brief moment of discomfort will benefit you by helping you combat your ex-partner's unwanted and inappropriate behaviors while co-parenting.

Examples of boundaries you might set include

- telling your ex-partner that you only want to communicate via text or email. This allows you to take time before responding and documents your interactions in case of future issues.

- communication boundaries such as your ex-partner only communicating with your child during certain hours of the day, via text or phone call, so that they don't disrupt your child's routine.

- being clear about what you expect from your ex-partner so that they can't make assumptions.

- firmly saying "no" and standing your ground when you don't want to do something your ex-partner is asking. This is especially vital if their request makes you uncomfortable, crosses one of your boundaries, or goes against the parenting plan.

Take note that these steps can also be used to create the boundaries you set with your extended family. It's also a good idea to help your child use this process to create their boundaries with their other parent.

Tips for Maintaining Boundaries

You may find that your ex-partner, and difficult extended family members, test your boundaries often. By reminding them of your boundaries and standing your ground, using the tips that follow, you ensure they understand that they cannot push you or your child around.

- Accept that your needs are important and setting boundaries communicates this to your ex-partner and extended family.

- Keep a written list of the boundaries you have set for yourself and your child that you can share with your ex-partner and extended family members when your child visits them.

- Be firm and clear using effective communication strategies to help your ex-partner understand that you will not accept unwanted behavior.

- Being assertive and consistent doesn't mean you're being rude. If your ex-partner (or extended family) has purposefully crossed a boundary, standing up for yourself protects you and your child from a repeat of the behavior in the future.

- Establishing consequences for when your boundaries are crossed ensures that your ex-partner and extended family know that crossing your or your child's boundaries will be taken seriously. These consequences may need to be included in your parenting plan to ensure that dangerous and serious behaviors have legal repercussions.

However, maintaining and enforcing your boundaries when your ex-partner has narcissistic tendencies requires effective communication.

Practicing Effective Communication

You're probably used to being told by your ex-partner that you're too sensitive or overreacting. They may even blame you for their mistakes and refuse to take responsibility for their actions. This can make communication challenging and result in one-sided conversations that make you feel invalidated and judged.

Fortunately, you don't have to put up with this. There are several communication strategies you can use to help you remain calm, ensure you're heard, and combat the challenges that arise. We'll take a look at three techniques that are especially helpful for communicating with an individual with narcissistic tendencies.

"I" Statements

These statements are useful for emphasizing your thoughts and needs without pointing out your ex-partner's flaws or negative behaviors—which could cause them to try and shut you down.

For example, you may want to shout that your ex-partner never listens to you when you try to talk to them about the parenting plan. This technique allows you to rephrase the sentence and say, "I feel that you didn't hear what I said about why I can't pick up [child's name] earlier than we agreed upon in the parenting plan."

This statement helps your ex-partner listen to what you're saying without resorting to negative behaviors because they feel attacked. Other examples of "I" statements include

- "I want..."
- "I feel..."
- "I wish..."
- "I hear..."

Active Listening

This technique helps you listen to your ex-partner to understand them and shows them they're being given your attention. Remember that narcissists thrive on attention, so this boosts the effectiveness of this strategy.

Take note that this activity is only helpful when your ex-partner is on the lower end of the spectrum of narcissism. If your ex-partner is higher on the spectrum or has hurt you or your child in the past, then you will need to make use of the Brief, Informative, Friendly, and Firm (BIFF) communication technique or opt for parallel parenting.

There are a few factors involved in being a good, active listener:

- Observe your ex-partner's nonverbal cues to identify the deeper meaning behind what is said. These cues include body language, tone of voice, and facial expressions.

- Remain fully present in the conversation to understand the content being communicated and the feeling of the underlying message.

- Use the above points to determine whether a response is appropriate and how to frame your response so that you can respond to what your ex-partner is actually trying to say.

- Reflect on what your ex-partner has told you by summarizing what they just said and repeating it back to them after paraphrasing it. This helps you ensure that you understand what is being communicated.

- Use open-ended questions that encourage a more detailed response instead of a simple yes or no answer. This shows your interest and helps your ex-partner provide better responses that allow you to communicate more effectively with each other. Examples of open-ended questions include

    - "Why do you think that?"

    - "Can you tell me more about [subject you're discussing]?"

- Remain neutral and withhold judgment while talking to your ex-partner to ensure they don't feel like they're being criticized, shamed, or blamed—three factors that could trigger negative reactions.

    - This could include taking a deep breath when you feel anger or frustration rise.

- Recognize what your ex-partner is saying, regardless of whether you agree with them.
- Use one of the communication strategies to respond (if a response is necessary).

The BIFF Communication Technique

BIFF is a type of communication technique that helps you manage difficult interactions using clear communication that won't trigger an emotional or unnecessary response from your ex-partner. This strategy is often used with individuals who exhibit high-conflict behavior, like narcissists. Using the BIFF technique, you can reduce conflict and emotional escalations. So, how does it work?

Brief

Your message should be short and leave out justifications and long explanations. This ensures your ex-partner only receives the information they need to fulfill their parenting responsibilities or solve a problem.

Informative

The information you provide should only include necessary information. This means leaving out accusations, emotions, and opinions. One way to determine if your message is informative is to ask whether your ex-partner can still respond or carry out their responsibilities without the phrase or sentence you aren't sure should be included.

Friendly

Your message should avoid emotional language while having a friendly and polite tone. You could also end the message with a short, positive, and neutral phrase like, "Best wishes."

Firm

Use a firm statement to end the conversation so that your ex-partner understands that you're serious and they cannot push you around. This may include offering two options for your ex-partner, decreasing the chances that they try to manipulate the situation to their advantage.

Scenario Example

You have to communicate the change in the schedule for your child's weekend visit to your ex-partner. Your original message may look as follows: "You always change the plans at the last minute. How can you behave so irresponsibly? It's unfair to our child and hurts them. You have to be considerate and stick to the schedule we both agreed on."

This first message will trigger your ex-partner and could lead to a fight. Using the BIFF technique, you can edit your message to one that won't cause conflict. For example, it could look like, "Hi [co-parent's name], I received your message regarding your work event on Saturday morning and wanted to discuss the change in this weekend's schedule. Thanks, [your name]."

Using Third-Party Communication Tools

Maintaining your boundaries and effectively communicating with someone who exhibits narcissistic tendencies can benefit from the use of third-party communication tools. They also act as a record of your interaction with your ex-partner and decrease the risk of confrontations that could lead to further harm.

You should choose the third-party platform by considering your and your ex-partner's needs, specific communication preferences, whether the interface is easy to use, how accessible the platform is, and the privacy and security measures implemented to safeguard your data and privacy. So, be sure to do your research. You can also speak with your lawyer about the options available, but the list that follows includes four of the most common platforms used by co-parents:

- AppClose

- Talking Parents
- Text messages
- Email

Managing Manipulation When Communicating

While setting boundaries and communicating effectively are vital to the co-parenting journey, manipulation tactics may still be used by your ex-partner to try and regain control. Let's take a look at the main types of manipulation tactics your ex-partner might use:

- **Gaslighting:** Phrases such as, "It wasn't that bad," and, "You're remembering it wrong," are used to deny your real experiences and shift blame away from your ex-partner.

- **Projection:** "You're so controlling," is one of the phases your ex-partner may use to project their feelings onto you. In this case, it's the narcissist that's controlling, not you.

- **Revenge seeking:** If your ex-partner feels you've wronged them, they may try and seek revenge using tactics like a smear campaign to destroy your reputation and isolate you.

- **Playing the victim:** Narcissists may try to gain sympathy and attention using phrases like, "Well, according to you, I can never do anything right."

- **Triangulation:** A phrase like, "Why can't you be more like [name of a third person]?" is used by narcissists to deflect your emotions and bring a third person into the situation that will support them.

- **Smear campaign:** Your ex-partner may try to discredit and isolate you using lies and exaggerations that they share with friends, family, your child's teachers, and anyone who will listen.

- **Guilt-tripping:** "I've done so much for you and you can't even do this one little thing for me," is meant to inspire guilt that coerces you into doing something you don't want to do but will benefit the narcissist.

Tips for Managing Manipulation

Besides setting and maintaining your boundaries and communicating effectively, you can also use the following tips to respond to manipulation tactics:

- Show yourself patience and self-compassion.

- Allow yourself to feel your emotions, recognize that the situation is not your fault, and take time for self-care.

- Step away and use the coping tools in this book to help you calm down and care for your mental well-being.

- Stay calm and choose what you will respond to to protect your mental and emotional well-being.

- Avoid contacting or interacting with your ex-partner unless it's necessary.

Manipulation is only one of the triggers of conflict between you and your ex-partner. You still need to develop a toolbox that will help you navigate conflict in a way that won't hurt your mental well-being or harm your child.

Action Steps

In this section, you'll find two activities that will help you practice the skills you've developed throughout this chapter.

Journaling to Process Emotions

Writing down your thoughts and feelings can provide you with a safe space to process your emotions without worrying that you will be judged. You can use the following journal prompts to help you start this process.

- If the emotions you're currently experiencing were a place, describe how they would feel, look, and sound.

- Choose one of your emotions and ask yourself "why" three times so that you can dive deeper into the reason behind this emotion.

- Write a letter to yourself with advice on how to manage the emotion and return to a state of calm. You can add to this letter as you work through the strategies in this book.

Practicing Effective Communication

Reflect on a past conversation with your ex-partner for this activity, or watch a short clip from a movie or show where a couple is arguing. Step into the shoes of one of the characters and respond to the other character using the following instructions:

1. How would you respond to the speaker using the BIFF technique? Write down your response.

2. Using the same scenario, create a response that uses the "I" statement technique.

Taking time to practice active listening helps you build the confidence needed to apply these techniques when communicating with your ex-partner. However, staying calm when conflict arises isn't always easy. So, you must continue building your skills by learning how to navigate disagreements and your ex-partner's hostile behavior.

Chapter 4:
Managing Conflict

Keep your cool in the face of conflict. Resilience means rising above the narcissistic games. –Di Stock

Co-parenting with an individual with narcissistic tendencies means you'll have to deal with conflict. Conflict can look different depending on your relationship with your ex-partner, but that doesn't mean its impact is any less serious. The strategies from the previous chapter are a great starting point for managing conflict, but now you need to add to your toolbox to protect your and your child's mental and emotional well-being.

High-Conflict Traits in Narcissists

You likely already know when and how conflict may arise on your co-parenting journey due to your relationship with your ex-partner. Understanding the four main categories of high-conflict behavior can help you further understand how conflict may rise and when.

- **All-or-nothing thinking:** Your ex-partner may see challenges as having only one solution. This prevents them from considering a compromise or finding other solutions better suited to the situation. When they believe the situation won't benefit them, they may react with extreme behaviors.

- **Blaming others:** It's easier for a narcissist to blame the people close to them than take responsibility for their behavior. This helps them feel like they have control over a situation or person, and frees them of the responsibility for a problem they likely caused or contributed to.

- **Unmanaged emotions:** Many narcissists struggle to manage their emotions using healthy coping mechanisms. Emotions may be experienced more intensely as a result, leading to harmful or violent behaviors, as well as other inappropriate reactions.

- **Extreme behaviors:** This behavior includes verbal, written, and physical actions that help the narcissist feel in control, meaning they will do what they can to retain this control over you. Threats and physical abuse are used as a way to prevent you from leaving them and controlling you.

High-conflict behaviors often form a predictable pattern. Developing the ability to notice and identify this pattern can help you prepare an appropriate response, or even avoid the situation—depending on the severity and danger of this pattern.

Interacting With a High-Conflict Person

Narcissists are often considered high-conflict individuals, but the severity of their behaviors will be unique. Co-parenting can make it challenging to avoid interactions with your ex-partner, so it's a good idea to have strategies available to guide you during interactions to prevent the conflict from escalating. This skill is also valuable if members of your extended family tend toward high-conflict behaviors.

The following tips can be used in conjunction with the strategies in the next section to guide you:

- Allow yourself to analyze the options available to you during a high-conflict situation. The option you choose should prioritize your and your child's physical, mental, and emotional safety.

- Limit the number of in-person interactions you and your child have with your ex-partner or high-conflict family members to limit exposure to these situations.
    - Take note that you may need to seek legal assistance, which could include a protection order, for family members that pose a danger to your and your child's well-being.

- Use the BIFF communication method to help you respond to your ex-partner, if a response is necessary, during these situations.

- Before interacting with your ex-partner or other high-conflict family members, list the types of behaviors you won't tolerate in your journal. This repeat of Chapter 1's exercise aims to help you enforce your and your child's boundaries and set a limit on the type of behavior that will be tolerated during challenging situations before legal assistance or law enforcement is contacted.

These techniques are a starting point for managing high-conflict behaviors, but they're not the only ones you could use.

Conflict Management Strategies

Your ex-partner may purposely start arguments over perceived slights or to re-establish control over you and your child. This can be frustrating, and you may get tired of it after having to go through it so many times. Gaslighting, blaming you for the situation, and other dangerous behaviors are often used during the conflict as well.

Since co-parenting means you won't always be able to avoid conflict with your ex-partner, you need to use strategies, like the ones discussed below, to anticipate conflict and deal with it in a way that won't escalate the situation or harm you.

Mindfulness for Anticipating Conflict

The first step to navigating any conflict is to remind yourself of what you can and cannot control. Refer back to Chapter 1's keys to resilience here. Once you've done that, you can begin developing your self-awareness. This allows you to anticipate what could trigger potential conflict so that you can mentally prepare for it. It's also valuable when conflict cannot be avoided. By learning how to purposefully use mindfulness, you develop the ability to shift your focus and stay in the present.

This makes it easier to fall back on healthy coping mechanisms to interact with your ex-partner. You could even decide that it's in your best interest to step away from the situation. You'll find a mindfulness meditation activity at the end of the chapter to help you start developing this skill.

Understanding Your Emotions in the Moment

While your ex-partner instigated the argument, identifying your emotions and understanding them can help you respond using helpful strategies. This prevents you from reacting in anger, leading to the situation escalating. Journaling and mindfulness activities, like the ones in this book, are a great starting point for developing your ability to identify and understand your emotions.

Step Back

Even when you have healthy coping skills and experience managing conflict, you may still need to step away from the situation so that you can calm down. Once calm, your mind will be clearer and allow you to think of resolutions to the conflict that won't harm you or your child. Stepping back is also valuable as it allows you to reassess your emotional and physical safety, and reset yourself by identifying what you need in the moment.

Consider Different Solutions

You and your ex-partner may have different motivations for wanting to make the final decision, but the final choice should be appropriate and account for your child's needs without harming either of you. In other words, you shouldn't be the only one to make sacrifices to reach a solution.

Take Responsibility for Your Behavior

You're not responsible for your ex-partner's narcissistic behaviors, but you are responsible for your behaviors and choices and how they impact your reactions. You can either respond calmly or react negatively like your ex-partner does. Your response can determine the outcome of the conflict, even if the solution is walking away and seeking guidance from your lawyer or a mediator.

Seek Out a Mediator

When conflict with your ex-partner cannot be resolved without outside help, you could consider seeking the guidance of an experienced person like a mediator. Mediators include lawyers, judges, counselors, psychologists, and professional mediators trained in managing conflict.

They provide a safe space where you and your ex-partner can work through the conflict and come to a solution. Assistance from a mediator can also help you seek a legally binding solution. This is helpful when your ex-partner has narcissistic tendencies and doesn't fulfill their co-parenting responsibilities.

Tips for Success

- Avoid directly confronting your ex-partner about their high-conflict behavior, as they will only shift tactics and won't change their view.

- Avoid talking about your feelings, as your ex-partner will lack the compassion needed to empathize with you. They may also weaponize them against you, leading to further harm.

- Avoid raising your voice, as it may lead to the situation escalating.

Navigating conflict when you are co-parenting is important, but it also puts your mental health at risk. So, how do you look after yourself during conflict?

Protecting Your Mental Health

Conflict of any kind can take a big toll on your mental health, but it can be especially harmful when your ex-partner has narcissistic tendencies.

The following section includes a few strategies you can use to take care of yourself.

Have Realistic Expectations

Your ex-partner's narcissistic behaviors can lead to them constantly disappointing you even when your expectations are already very low. And constant disappointment can have a very negative impact on your mental health.

Take time to reflect on your expectations for your ex-partner on the co-parenting journey. Then re-evaluate these expectations so that they are more realistic. You could even list these expectations in your journal to keep track of them and review them before interacting with your ex-partner.

Keep a Journal

Writing down your emotions, thoughts, and experiences gives you a safe space to vent without worrying about judgment. This can also help you work through negative thoughts, prioritize your concerns and fears, and track triggers caused by the trauma your ex-partner inflicted.

Meditation

This relaxing activity can help you manage stress and practice mindfulness. It can help you notice negative thoughts and tension in your body, and work through challenges, allowing you to practice staying in the present moment and become more self-aware.

Prayer

If you're spiritual or religious, you can read through scripture, quotes, or passages that hold meaning to you. This can mentally, emotionally, and spiritually support and empower you during challenging moments.

It can also provide you with the support you may need to work through difficult moments.

Get Creative

Embracing your hobbies and getting creative, regardless of your skill, is a great way to relieve stress. This activity can even be meditative. Adult coloring books, painting, using a hobby kit, or any other creative activity can help you step away from the stress in your life and relax.

Move Your Body

You don't have to get a gym membership or run a marathon, but moving your body every day, even for short periods, can benefit your mental and emotional health. Running, walking, swimming, cycling, yoga, and hiking are just a few suggestions. If you aren't sure what you might enjoy, try out different activities first.

Seek Professional Help

Conflict with a narcissist can be extremely harmful to your mental health. Seeking help from a professional can help you work through the hurt that you've had to deal with from your ex-partner, as well as the resulting trauma. A mental health professional can also help you build self-confidence and become mentally stronger.

These activities can be added to your daily schedule through experimentation. You may find that you have time for a short mindfulness meditation every morning before work. Or perhaps you could work on your hobby while your child watches an episode of their favorite program. Even going on short walks with your child can be beneficial.

Action Steps

Many activities could be added to your daily routine to help you care for your mental health. In this section, you'll find three activities that help you get started.

Gratitude Activity

List three to five things you're grateful for every day in your journal, from the smile your child gave you before going to school to the weather being perfect for a relaxing walk. The little things that make your day good can empower you to remember that your ex-partner doesn't get to make your life miserable.

Three-Minute Mindfulness

1. Sit down on your couch, the floor, or your bed.
2. Set your phone's timer to three minutes.
3. Close your eyes and focus on your breathing.
4. Breathe in slowly through your nose and allow the air to fill your stomach, pushing it out.
5. Hold your breath for a count of one second.
6. Breathe out through your mouth, allowing the air to deflate your stomach. Make your exhale longer than your inhale.
7. Repeat this breathing pattern until your timer rings.

Progressive Muscle Relaxation

Once you're comfortable practicing the previous activity, add the following steps:

1. As you breathe, purposefully relax the muscles in your face.

2. During your next breath, release the tension in your neck and shoulders.

3. Repeat this process until you've purposefully relaxed all the muscles in your body, including the ones in your toes.

Navigating conflict while co-parenting means learning to choose your battles and deciding what's best for your and your child's mental health and well-being. You also show your child that it's important that they prioritize themselves to cope with their other parent's behavior. However, there is another form of conflict that could arise due to your ex-partner trying to use your child to hurt you.

Chapter 5:
Addressing Parental Alienation

Alienation aims to divide, but resilient co-parenting seeks to heal and reunite. –Di Stock

Manipulative and coercive tactics can take many forms. To a narcissist, they're seen as the key to acquiring attention, power, and control. Arming yourself with an understanding of how these tactics are practiced gives you the power to combat them. While we've discussed many of the manipulative tactics your ex-partner may use against you in previous chapters, it's time to understand how they may try to weaponize your child against you. We'll also look at the strategies you can use to protect your child and fight back against your ex-partner without confronting them.

Identifying Parental Alienation

After separating from or divorcing your ex-partner, your contact with each other is minimal. This can empower you to deny your ex-partner the control they had over you and your child. However, once your ex-partner realizes this separation leads to a lack of control and power, they may attempt to regain it by adjusting their coercive and manipulative tactics to suit the new situation—possibly leading to more abuse and cruel behavior.

This is when parental alienation may arise. One parent, your ex-partner, may use their anger at or hatred of you to pressure your child into rejecting and hating you—even if those aren't their true feelings. The effect this has on you and your child can be emotionally and mentally harmful. Parental alienation occurs on three main levels:

- **Mild:** Your child is resistant to spending time with you but does enjoy your time together once your ex-partner has left.

- **Moderate:** Resistance begins to increase, and you may struggle to contact your child. They may also begin to display additional behaviors of opposition, like defiance and a lack of cooperation.

- **Severe:** This level can lead to such extreme resistance that your child may attempt to avoid you or run away.

Depending on the severity of parental alienation, your child may feel neglected and angry, possibly taking on the traits (like poor empathy and rigid thinking) of your ex-partner to cope with the situation. This could also lead to

- problems at school.

- difficulties establishing and maintaining relationships in the future.

- mental health problems like depression, guilt, anxiety, and delinquent behavior.

- poor self-esteem and lack of self-respect.

You'll have to deal with the impact of your child suddenly treating you negatively, including the feelings of loss, helplessness, anger, anxiety, and frustration that may arise. Your child may also exhibit these negative behaviors with other family members and friends, leading to further alienation that gives your ex-partner a better sense of power and control.

However, parental alienation isn't the only challenge you and your child may have to deal with. Loyalty conflicts may start to arise even before you and your ex-partner have officially separated. This is when your child believes they'll need to choose between you and your ex-partner.

Loyalty conflicts often arise when your ex-partner argues with you or openly exhibits narcissistic behaviors like diminishing your accomplishments and experiences. Even subtle criticism performed purposefully in front of your child to get them to choose a side can begin to negatively affect both of you.

To cope, your child may start to behave like two different people when spending time with you and your ex-partner. Poor self-esteem, out-of-character behavior (like acting more aggressively), and anxiety often arise as a result. But what are the signs of parental alienation?

Common Symptoms

Several common signs of parental alienation exist. You can use these signs to help you identify it.

What signs could your child exhibit?

- They may openly disapprove of the decisions you make and your behaviors.

- Your ex-partner may be seen as perfect by your child.

- Hostile behaviors and negative or defiant attitudes may be justified by your child.

- Your child may not display visible guilt for their actions.

- Your extended family may be shown hostile behaviors.

- Your child may adopt the opinions, behaviors, and actions of your ex-partner.

What signs might your ex-partner exhibit?

- They may attempt to limit the contact you have with your child.

- You may be openly criticized and insulted by your ex-partner.

- It may be challenging to obtain your child's vital academic, medical, and other information from your ex-partner.

- Your ex-partner may interfere with your communication with your child, twisting your words and messages to suit their needs.

- They may tell your child that you're dangerous and don't have their best interests in mind.

- Your ex-partner may convince your child that you don't love them.

- Your child may be forced to choose between you and your ex-partner (also known as a "loyalty conflict").

What Can You Do?

Parental alienation can be extremely harmful to you, your child, and the rest of your family. In the next section, we'll discuss specific strategies for helping you combat alienation, but let's look at a few important tips first.

- **Keep records of everything.** You may have to pursue legal action to combat parental alienation. Make a record of your interactions with your child and their behavior; your ex-partner's words and actions; copies of text messages, emails, and other communication between you, your child, and your ex-partner; and accounts of events like arguments. You can dedicate a journal solely to this task so that all your information is kept in one place.

- **Speak with other adults in your child's life.** Family members, the parents of your child's friends, teachers, coaches, and counselors are all individuals who can provide you with feedback about any changes in your child's behavior. They can also act as witnesses if you do pursue legal action.

- **Get legal advice.** Parental alienation can lead to serious false accusations that can be extremely harmful to you and your child. Seeking help from a qualified lawyer can help you combat further damage and ensure that your ex-partner will no longer harm you or your child.

- **Consider seeking help from a psychologist or a counselor.** The psychological and emotional impact of parental alienation can be extremely damaging to you and your child, as well as your relationship. Additionally, everyone's situation is unique. Seeking personalized help from a qualified individual can help you and your child heal from the damage, rebuild your relationship, and combat further harm from your ex-partner.

Keep in mind that your ex-partner may not truly care about your child or how their behavior affects them. Your child may simply be seen as a tool that allows your ex-partner to stay in control. Seek help from sources like lawyers and psychologists in addition to the strategies discussed in the next section.

Strategies for Countering Alienation

You don't have to stand by and allow your child to be used like a tool. You can take control of the situation and implement a variety of strategies, like the ones discussed here, to help you combat parental alienation and remind your child that they are important to you no matter what your ex-partner or other family members tell them

Listen to Your Child

Regardless of your child's age, it's important that you make time in your daily schedule to give them your full attention and listen to what they have to say. This activity could occur before school, after school, or before bedtime—this will depend on your child. Give them the space to vent their emotions without having to worry about being judged, questioned, or criticized. Be sure to also ask your child if they only want you to listen or if they would like you to offer solutions if they share a problem with you.

Practice Patience

It can be hard, but sometimes children only want us to listen as they vent their emotions. This means inviting your child to ask questions, make comments, and share their experiences and emotions. But avoid pressuring them to share, as this could lead to unintended alienation. Instead, allow them to come to you when they're ready.

Don't Break Your Promises

No matter how small, do your best to always be on time and follow through on any promises you make to your child.

Don't Become Defensive

Dealing with your ex-partner's narcissistic tendencies can make it challenging not to justify your actions to your child or share how your ex-partner has hurt you. But it's not your child's responsibility to be your friend or support network. They don't have the emotional skills or mental capacity to do so. Instead, seek out members in your support network.

Build the Relationship With Time, Fun, and Positivity

Purposefully spending time with your child, even if you're playing video games together at home, can be extremely beneficial for developing your relationship with them. It's also helpful to listen as they talk about their interests even if you don't understand why it's so important to them.

Don't Play the Blame Game

Your child may be coerced by your ex-partner to spy on you, but this isn't their fault. It can also be harmful to vent your frustration and anger at your ex-partner where your child can hear you. So, avoid blaming your ex-partner or criticizing them when your child is around.

Use Positive Language

The language used to communicate with your child is important. This could look like stepping into your child's shoes and thinking like them. So, phrases like the following can be changed to ones that have a positive impact:

- Change, "I miss you," to, "I look forward to seeing you next time!"
- Change, "I wish I could see that," to, "Woah, that's so great to hear. You must have been very excited."

Remind Your Child You Love Them

When in contact with your child, in person or over the phone, tell them you love and care about them. Your child can't read your mind—reminding them that you love them, are proud of them, and that you think about them often can have a positive impact on their emotional well-being.

Be Yourself

You may try to be the perfect parent to counteract your ex-partner's narcissistic and alienating behaviors, but this could further alienate your child. Instead, act as you always have. You have your child's best interests in mind and don't need to try and act extra special to be the caring, kind, and supportive parent you've always been.

Lean on Your Support Network

Your support network will be crucial for helping you cope with the mental, emotional, and physical challenges that accompany parental alienation. They can listen to you vent, help you work out challenging situations, and offer support during this difficult time.

The above strategies are also valuable for helping you combat alienation from extended family. However, if your extended family has shown you support but is being shut out by your child, work through these strategies with them so that your child's relationship with their extended family isn't irrevocably harmed by your ex-partner. This could look like sleepovers at their grandparents or movie nights with their aunt, for example.

Putting It Into Practice

This activity will be short as you're simply putting the information from this chapter into practice using the following instructions as your guide.

The Journaling Record

1. Start by buying a journal and a file that you can dedicate to recording your interactions with your child and ex-partner.

2. Begin making frequent entries that detail your emotions, changes in your child's behavior, the circumstances surrounding the event you're journaling about, and copies of text messages

or other evidence you can keep in the file to support these entries.

Creating Special Traditions With Your Child

1. In your journal, list the activities you and your child like to do alone and together.

2. Pick one activity and turn it into a special tradition you can practice when they spend time with you.

    A. For example, you could dedicate the first Friday of every month to going to the movies or having a movie night at home with their favorite snacks.

    B. You could also dedicate Sunday mornings to having a special breakfast with your child.

There's no right or wrong way to practice the above activities. They are simply a starting point for helping you build your relationship with your child so that if your ex-partner does practice parental alienation tactics, you're prepared to take action quickly. This brings us to one of the most crucial topics in co-parenting: Planning your finances and being prepared to take legal action.

Chapter 6:
Legal and Financial Planning

Secure your co-parenting journey with sound legal and financial strategies. Protect your peace and your future. –Di Stock

Navigating the legal and financial aspects of co-parenting can be overwhelming and distressing. Fortunately, building your knowledge base and doing additional research can arm you with the tools you need to thrive. You can also seek additional help using the resources in Appendix A.

By building your knowledge base, you also empower yourself. This is great for helping you build confidence as you rebuild your life. We'll start by building on what we learned in Chapter 2 about parental rights and responsibilities.

Traversing the Legal System

While you and your ex-partner need to fulfill your parental rights and responsibilities after divorce, they may still change. Changes depend on the type of custody and visitation arrangements made during the divorce process and when further legal action is pursued to protect yourself and your child against further harm from your ex-partner.

Two main types of custody often occur during divorce. Joint legal custody, also called "shared legal custody" or "shared parental responsibility," provides you and your ex-partner with shared authority over your child's well-being. However, your relationship with your ex-partner may make it impossible to make decisions together because of their narcissistic tendencies. So, sole custody may be a better option since it gives you full authority over decisions relating to your child's well-being.

Your custody arrangement will also be adjusted to suit your specific situation. Judges make these adjustments according to the custody and parental laws of your country and state. Speaking with your lawyer and doing your own research can combat the fear that may arise during this process, as you'll be armed with the knowledge you need to make informed decisions and feel more comfortable and confident during legal activities.

Navigating Court Proceedings

The following factors should be considered when preparing for court activities:

- **Research how child custody works in your country and state.** Child custody practices differ depending on the country and state you live in. Factors you need to pay special attention to include custodial rights, paternity laws (if you and your ex-partner weren't married), the definitions of custody for your country and state, and other legal terminology used in family court.

- **Work with a lawyer.** If you can, work with a lawyer as they can help you create a parenting plan, identify and gather the evidence you'll need, prepare and file the necessary paperwork, and help you prepare your responses to questions you're asked in court.

- **Gather evidence.** Evidence is the most crucial part of a custody case, especially if your ex-partner has physically or emotionally abused you and your child. Examples of documents that can be collected as evidence include medical reports and criminal records, copies of messages between you and your ex-partner, photos and videos of you and your child, and your journal entries. You should also include any information that supports whether your child will be safe with extended family members.

- **Find witnesses.** Relatives, friends, medical doctors, teachers, and mental health professionals are all witnesses who can back up your claims in court and provide firsthand knowledge of the type of relationship you have with your child.

- **Create your parenting plan.** You'll find sources for parenting plan templates in Appendix A. Use them to guide you in creating this plan correctly so that you can take it to court. You can add custom rules to account for your ex-partner's narcissistic behaviors and schedule how much time is given to each parent and different extended family members depending on your custody arrangement.

- **Stay organized.** There's a lot of information involved in court proceedings. Work with your lawyer to familiarize yourself with this information and stay organized. This could include drafting several versions of your parenting plan to help you figure out what does and doesn't work for you before your lawyer looks at it.

- **Be prepared.** Familiarize yourself with court procedures, with your lawyer's guidance, before going to court. You can ask your lawyer or another court employee about the order of proceedings and who will be in the courtroom.

Keep in mind that the role of your extended family members should also be considered when creating your parenting plan and negotiating custody arrangements. If extended family members don't pose any physical, mental, or emotional danger to your child, they may be granted specific visitation and custody rights that meet your family's needs. This benefits your child as they are guaranteed time with people who love them. And if extended family members do pose a danger, these arrangements will help you protect your child from them and your ex-partner.

This leads us to the court hearing. The procedures of these hearings will differ depending on your country and state, but extra research and talking to your lawyer can help you familiarize yourself with these proceedings. This minimizes the anxiety and uncertainty of an already challenging process.

Tips for Court Appearances

While family court processes do differ, the following list of tips can be used to help you prepare:

- **Arrive early.** Arriving at least 30 minutes to 1 hour before your hearing begins allows you to account for parking challenges and unexpected traffic, use the bathroom, and talk to your attorney before you enter the courtroom.

- **Leave your child in the care of a trusted adult.** This can make it easier to focus solely on what's happening in the courtroom and protects your child from any negative behaviors your ex-partner displays on the day.

- **Plan ahead and practice patience.** You may end up waiting for a few hours after your originally scheduled time before entering the courtroom, depending on how busy the court is that day. Pack a water bottle and snack to make this waiting period more comfortable.

- **Speak with your attorney to understand what will happen.** Your attorney should inform you about the processes that will take place, what will be expected of you, how you should dress, and how you should behave.

- **Be respectful to all members of the court, especially the judge.** All members of the court, even your ex-partner's lawyer, should be shown respect as your behavior in court can affect how the judge sees you. If you have to tell your lawyer something urgent, write it down and slide the paper over to them. Be sure to keep your phone on silent as well.

- **Speak with your attorney immediately after the hearing.** Taking a moment to reflect on what happened in the courtroom with your lawyer can help you understand what happens next. This is especially helpful if the judge has taken the opportunity to first think about everything presented to them before moving to make a decision.

These tips can help you manage any anxiety and fear that may arise at the prospect of going to court. After all, this process can be scary. Trust in your lawyer and remind yourself that remaining informed, calm, and patient will give a good impression to the court and help you navigate the court system with determination and perseverance.

This brings us to the next crucial topic in separating from and divorcing your ex-partner: Taking charge of your financial future.

Financial Planning Before, During, and After Divorce

Planning your finances and working toward financial independence after separating from someone with narcissistic tendencies is crucial. However, you may experience anxiety about finances after ending your relationship. While you don't have to become a financial expert, building your knowledge and having a basic understanding of finances is crucial to making informed financial decisions that benefit your and your child's future.

This also protects your family's long-term well-being and can combat the anxiety and fear that arise from your new financial situation due to divorce. Appendix A has several financial resources you can use, and the section that follows will provide you with essential tips for starting your journey.

Securing Financial Independence

Gaining financial independence, especially from a narcissist, can provide you with a new sense of freedom. But you still have to create a budget that covers your and your child's financial needs and helps you work toward new financial goals that will secure your future. The following list discusses the factors you need to consider to help you pursue financial independence.

- **Collect your financial documents.** These documents include your bank statements, tax returns, investment accounts, retirement accounts, loans you've taken, credit cards, property deeds, and prenuptial and postnuptial agreements. These documents will form the foundation of planning your finances.

- **Calculate your income and new expenses.** Calculate your total income using all your streams of income. Then list and calculate all your current expenses, including debts you're paying off. This provides insight into your current financial needs. Additionally, list any divorce expenses you have to pay.

- **Use this information to calculate your new budget.** Appendix A has several templates for building a new budget. You will do this using all the information you've gathered so far. Remember that your budget will help you create a financial roadmap to achieving stability and independence. You can also use your budget to set new long-term and short-term financial goals.

- **Rebuild your emergency fund.** You may have either dipped into this fund or had it split between you and your ex-partner during divorce. Making it a goal to rebuild this fund is crucial to ensuring you are financially supported during any type of emergency.

- **Close your joint accounts.** Any accounts you and your ex-partner shared should be closed to prevent future problems or financial entanglements. Instead, open new accounts in your name to ensure you are the only one with access to your money. Be sure to update your life insurance policies and wills to match your new circumstances and custody agreements as well.

You could also consider seeking financial guidance. A financial planner can help you navigate legal and financial complexities after divorce, but you can also seek out budgeting services. There are many online financial support resources and companies you could work with too. Just be sure that the company you choose is qualified to navigate the financial aspects and laws specific to the country and state you live in.

As you can see, it's possible to take back control of your financial future and feel secure again. Asking for help while doing this can also be extremely beneficial for combating any anxiety you may have about finances. But this doesn't mean you won't feel panicked or anxious during legal or financial activities. So what do you do?

Practicing Grounding

Anxiety can quickly creep up when you have to go to court or work on finances. Learning to ground yourself in the moment can help you work through your fear and anxiety so that you can continue your journey. In this section, you'll find an activity to help you ground yourself when you start feeling anxious or panicked.

Grounding With Your Senses

This activity can help you calm down and exit your panicked state using your five senses. Name five things that you can

1. Hear

2. See

3. Touch (from where you're sitting or standing)

4. Smell

5. Taste

Grounding With Water

If you're at home, you can add another grounding activity:

1. Place your hands into either a bowl of water or under a running tap.

2. Focus on the temperature of the water.

3. Notice how the water feels on your palms, fingertips, and the back of your hands.

Now that you have all the tools you need to navigate co-parenting, we can start looking at the strategies that will help you build a positive and safe home environment where you and your child will thrive.

Part 3:

Family-Focused Strategies

In the heart of every strong family are strategies that nurture resilience and love. –Di Stock

Chapter 7:
Fostering Emotional Safety and Creating a Positive Home Environment

Be the calm in THEIR storm. Build a home where your kids always feel safe. –Di Stock

We are now going to shift our focus to building a healthier and more positive home environment for your child. The strategies that will be discussed aren't difficult, and you can easily adapt them to suit your lifestyle. In Chapter 8, we'll focus on specific techniques that target different age groups. For now, let's focus on the key methods for fostering emotional safety and building a positive home environment—a process that starts with the creation of a routine.

The Value of Establishing Routines

Routines are a great way to create stability for you and your child after a life-changing event like divorce. This stability helps your child feel safe and know what to expect as you move forward. And by decreasing the uncertainty in their life, you lower the risk of behavioral issues.

In general, a routine can be defined as the scheduled activities occurring in the mornings, after school, and before bed. While they may be slightly flexible, routines consist of activities that occur in a specific order every day.

Routines are extremely valuable tools for providing stability as they act as a way to build a sense of belonging and togetherness, and they allow you and your child to connect and share things. Additionally, the predictability of a routine creates a sense of safety and belonging that is vital for combating the anxiety that may arise due to unpredictable events like divorce, puberty, and moving house.

You will also benefit from the establishment of routines. They can build your confidence in your parenting skills, help you feel organized and in control during unpredictable moments, and make it easier to make decisions and get through tasks quickly so that you can use your spare time for other things, like bonding with your child or making time for self-care.

The activity at the end of this chapter will help you develop a routine that meets your family's specific needs and lifestyle. But before we continue, let's take a look at a few tips for helping your child cope with change.

Helping Your Child Adapt to Change

Chapter 10 will dive into greater detail on the specific strategies you can use to help your child develop resilience. This will equip them with the skills they need to endure change throughout their lives. For now, you can use the following tips to guide you in helping your child adapt.

Help Your Child Grieve the Divorce

You can use the steps for grieving a relationship in Chapter 11 as a guide to helping your child grieve the divorce. During this process, keep in mind that your divorce may be felt as intensely as the death of a loved one. Your child is going to need time to process the changes and new circumstances.

In addition to talking to them about the divorce, you should also listen to your child when they're ready to talk. Allow them to be honest about their feelings without worrying about repercussions, even if you don't agree with them or feel hurt by them, and acknowledge that their emotions are valid.

While you shouldn't confide in your child like you would a friend, you can be honest and let them know that you're also hurting, but these feelings aren't forever, and you will both find healing and happiness.

Provide Love and Constant Reassurance

Children are remarkably resilient and can heal quickly when given love, support, and attention. However, this is only possible if your actions, words, and abilities consistently reinforce that you will be there for your child. This means reassuring them that you love them; telling them that things might not be easy right now, but they will be okay; and offering your child physical reassurance using hugs and quality time.

Tell Your Child It's Not Their Fault

Children often believe that their parent's divorce is their fault. You know this isn't true, but your child doesn't. It's important that you sit down with your child and talk to them about the divorce (these strategies are discussed in Chapter 10). Be patient too. Remember that your child doesn't have as much experience in the world or relationships as you do.

Be sure to implement the above tips alongside the information throughout this book to create a truly effective strategy. Now we will dive into the principles you can use to create a positive home environment where your child feels safe, loved, and supported.

Building a Nurturing and Supportive Atmosphere

Another goal you may have is to create a home environment that nurtures and supports your child. This activity provides several benefits, including fostering emotional well-being and a better relationship between you and your child. The following principles can help you start this process:

- **Show your child affection.** Regular physical affection can help you strengthen your emotional connection with your child due to the release of oxytocin, also called the "I love you" hormone. Depending on your child's age, you can ask them what type of affection they're comfortable with receiving. This ensures you respect their boundaries and emphasizes the importance of consent before someone touches them or enters their personal space. The goal is to parent with focus and intention.

- **Be emotionally and physically present.** This is crucial for creating stability and ensuring your child knows you support and love them. Active listening and being available to your child, even when you don't have full conversations, can be vital for ensuring they share their feelings and ask you for help.

- **Encourage healthy habits.** Remember that your child watches you and will likely imitate your behaviors. Practicing healthy habits, having a good sleep routine, and making time for self-care (as discussed in later chapters) all benefit your child too.

- **Practice positive and consistent discipline.** Misbehavior can help you gain insight into your child's current emotions. Use this as an opportunity to reconnect with your child, help them learn from the natural consequences of their actions, and understand what they may be struggling with (mentally and emotionally).

- **Use mindfulness to find balance and welcome change.** The goal is to find a balance that ensures your child understands that you value spending time with them, even if you both have one or two free hours (depending on their age) where you can both do activities on your own.

Now that you have a starting point, you can take the next step. This means using your words and actions to show your child that you care.

Conveying a Nurturing Attitude

Encouraging positive behavior in your child, creating stability, and strengthening your relationship with each other can be achieved by developing a positive approach to your parenting. The following tips will help you influence your child's behavior in a way that will benefit them.

Encourage Your Child

Knowing they have your support, even if you don't completely understand the hobby or activity they're working on, helps your child feel comfortable opening up to you and seeking your guidance. If their other parent's narcissistic tendencies are hurting your child, you'll not only identify this issue early but also combat it by validating your child's skills and love for the activity.

Practice Active Listening and Respond to Cues

Active listening may not always be useful in your co-parenting relationship, but this practice can still benefit your relationship with your child. Using your body language and the active listening strategies from previous chapters, you can ensure your child feels they are being heard without being judged.

It's also important to be mindful of your child's communication signals so you can respond appropriately. This helps build trust and a sense of security, strengthening your bond with your child.

Use a Nonjudgmental Attitude

The key to ensuring your child sees you as a safe place is to practice a nonjudgmental attitude. Ensuring you are seen as a safe place can help you determine whether your child is still safe or if they need professional help. It allows you to protect your child by identifying the early warning signs of abuse.

Effectively Setting Expectations

While you want your home to be a safe, positive, and supportive environment, you should still set expectations. Expectations act as guidelines that children can use to work toward long- and short-term goals. This includes understanding what type of behavior is expected from them in different situations and the consequences of misbehaving. You have to openly and honestly communicate your expectations with your child. They should also be fair and reasonable. Remember, they're still children.

The tips that follow can be used as a guide for setting expectations:

- Expectations should be realistic and account for your child's age, needs, strengths, and weaknesses.

- Remind yourself that your child is a unique individual who is developing at their own rate. Avoid comparing them to your younger self and other children.

- Avoid projecting your personal challenges and expectations onto your child.

- Consistency is key to ensuring your child understands what's expected of them. This means practicing patience and being prepared to calmly remind your child and correct them when they do break the rules.

- Celebrate your child's achievements, no matter how small. This helps them stay motivated to continue working toward their goals, while also acknowledging the hard work they've already put in.

Examples of Potential Bonding Activities

There are many ways to bond with your child. Every child is different, and their experiences with your ex-partner may mean that the strategies that work for someone else's child don't work for your child. Don't be afraid to experiment and tailor these activities according to your child's interests and needs, as they will likely be the most successful strategies. You can find a few examples in this section to get started.

- Eat breakfast and dinner together.
- Spend time playing or working on a hobby with your child.

- Make time before bed to talk about what happened that day and use open-ended questions like, "What made you laugh today?" to encourage them to open up.

- Build responsibility and connect with your child by allowing them to help with chores like cleaning up after dinner or packing away laundry.

- Write a short note that wishes your child a good day and reminds them you love them, and pack it into their schoolbag or lunchbox.

- Play is one of the best ways to build and strengthen the bond with your child and encourage emotional expression, so make time to play with them.
  - You could play board games, have a tea party, play with building blocks, or play outside.
  - Games will change depending on your child's age and what they're interested in.

Allow yourself to be flexible and try out different activities, especially since children often have shifting interests. It's also a good idea to ask your child what they would like to do with you.

Action Steps

A good routine is well-planned so that everyone understands what is expected of them and when, and it should be regular so that it becomes part of everyday life. Your routine should also be predictable. This means tasks are generally completed in the same order every time, making it easy for younger children to practice too.

In this activity, you're going to start building a routine that works for your family. Simply follow the steps below to get started:

1. Create a column for each demanding part of the day. For example, your columns could have the following headings: Morning, after school, dinner time, and bedtime.

2. List the activities that would be completed under each heading.

    A. Try to organize these activities into the exact steps they're completed in. For example, the morning routine could be listed as: Wake up, brush your teeth, wash your face, brush your hair, and get dressed.

    B. Listing the activities as simple steps prevents you and your child from becoming overwhelmed by information.

3. Add in any chores that your child is responsible for under each heading.

4. Designate time specifically for connecting with your child. This could include playtime or spending time together.

5. Use a posterboard, a whiteboard, or any other large visualizer to create a more organized and easy-to-read version of each routine.

6. Hang the visual form of the routine in an area of the home where you and your child can easily view it.

7. If your child needs to check off activities to ensure they've been completed each day, alter the routine board. For example,

    A. Use a whiteboard so that your child can tick off each activity every day.

    B. Have a key chain with different colored bangles attached to it.

        i. Each color should represent one activity on the routine board.

        ii. When the activity is completed, the correct colored bangle should be taken off the key chain and hung on a hook attached to the routine board to indicate the activity was completed.

8. Take note that as your child gets older, this routine will need to change. You can also begin involving your child in the creation of the adjusted routine (depending on their age) so they can begin developing teamwork skills.

The information from this chapter has provided you with a solid foundation for rebuilding your life and developing your relationship with your child. But you may wonder how you can adapt these techniques to meet your child's needs according to their age. Turn the page to find out.

Chapter 8:

Understanding Your Child's Needs

Know your child, know their needs. That's how you win at co-parenting. –Di Stock.

Your family may be considered high-conflict due to your ex-partner's narcissistic tendencies and behaviors. In situations where co-parenting is possible, children will still have their physical, emotional, and mental needs met.

Keep in mind, however, that if you and your child have experienced abuse or are not safe around your ex-partner, then it's better to opt for alternative methods, like parallel and solo parenting, and to seek guidance from your lawyer and an experienced counselor or psychologist. But how do you and your ex-partner adapt to your child's ever-changing needs as they get older?

Co-Parenting During Developmental Stages

A child's needs are constantly changing as they get older. Regardless of your child's current age, you and your ex-partner need to be prepared to adapt to meet these needs while presenting a united front.

This can be a challenge when your ex-partner is a narcissist, that's why you need to make use of tools like a parenting plan and the strategies in this book to build resilience and navigate your co-parenting relationship in a way that suits your situation.

The goal is to be consistent in your parenting strategies to provide stability, support, and safety to your child despite the narcissistic behaviors of your ex-partner. Let's take a look at a few of the most vital ways you can do this during each stage of development.

Infants Aged 0 to 1 Year Old

Your focus will be on helping your child develop a secure attachment using consistent and nurturing techniques. This includes establishing a predictable routine that allows you and your ex-partner to meet your child's needs and respond to them quickly. The predictability of the routine will also create a sense of safety and trust for your child when they move between the two homes.

Frequent face-to-face interactions and skin-to-skin contact will be valuable as well. You should also ensure that your child's environment is calm and consistent, and that their contact with you and your ex-partner is safe and predictable.

Toddlers Aged 1 to 2 Years Old

Continue ensuring your child's environment is safe for them to explore so that they can begin developing their confidence and establishing independence. Being fully present during your child's playtime also helps your child feel safe and cared for.

A consistent routine is still crucial for decreasing anxiety and preventing confusion. When you need to explain things to prevent uncertainty, use clear and simple language that's adapted to your child's level of understanding. You'll also need to model healthy emotional expressions and behaviors you'd like to see as toddlers learn by observing their parents.

Toddlers Aged 2 to 3 Years Old

In addition to consistent routines, make time to engage in play with your child. This helps them develop social skills, strengthens your bond with them, reinforces their sense of security, and encourages them to explore their world.

Consistent affection like cuddling and hugs establishes a sense of security and love. You'll also need to expand your child's emotional vocabulary by labeling feelings when you read picture books, draw, play, or during everyday activities.

Comfort items, like specific toys and blankets, that travel with your child between the two homes can bring comfort and security during transition periods. Ensuring the home environment is safe for exploration is also crucial for reinforcing their confidence and independence. Continue modeling and teaching healthy emotional expression as well. But adjust the language you use to explain things to your child so that fits their understanding.

Take note that children learn by watching their parents, and they're highly intuitive. So, it's important to minimize your child's exposure to conflict and negative language between you and your ex-partner. Instead, opt for positive or neutral language around your ex-partner and when you talk about them. This can protect your child from stress and avoid confusion about your relationship with your ex-partner.

Preschoolers Aged 3 to 5 Years Old

Rapid emotional, physical, mental, and social development will continue during this stage. You'll notice that your child is starting to communicate more and form connections with other children while exercising their independence too.

You'll need to continue developing your child's emotional skills as a result. Teaching them to recognize and name their emotions using picture books, emotion cards, and stories, and talking to them can help you do this. You can also start playing role-play games with your child. These games teach your child skills like sharing, expressing empathy, and learning to take turns by acting out different scenarios and their possible responses.

Additionally, helping your child manage their emotions during this stage could include teaching them to practice deep breathing and counting to 10. Drawing, storytelling, and physical activities are a few extra strategies you could use.

Your parenting plan will also need to be adjusted to meet these changing needs. This could include altered routines, scheduling playdates with other children, and ensuring the extended family can spend time with your child.

You'll have to continue thoughtfully managing any conflict that arises as well, including protecting your child from witnessing negative interactions and disagreements between you and your ex-partner.

School Children Aged 6 to 8 Years

As school becomes more academically and socially challenging for your child, you will need to collaborate more with your ex-partner about any challenges your child may be facing at school. This includes creating a connection with your child's teachers and school faculty, like counselors. You will also need to inform your child's school about your family's parenting agreements, as well as any challenges your child may be facing due to the separation or divorce.

Continue developing your child's confidence and competence as well. This can be done by assigning them age-appropriate responsibilities like chores. Children aged 6 to 8 could be asked to pack their toys into their toy bin after playtime. This can also help foster a sense of independence.

Strong social skills and learning to develop healthy relationships with their peers are also important. These connections can significantly impact a child's emotional and social development, especially during times of family stress like separation.

Create stability and security, while also providing the opportunity for social connection, by having your child join a club or group activity for something they enjoy doing. Setting up playdates can also be valuable for supporting a child's social connections.

School Children Aged 9 to 12 Years Old

Helping your child safely develop and practice their independence as they approach their teenage years is vital. This period allows you to teach them critical-thinking and decision-making skills, while also developing their self-reliance—skills crucial to coping when one parent has narcissistic tendencies.

During this stage, it's important to have age-appropriate discussions with your child. Encourage them to join conversations, share their thoughts, and offer ideas. This includes creating an environment where your child feels free to express their feelings. Supporting your child's emotions, helping them understand them, and teaching your child how to handle emotions healthily all play a role in this.

Activities like deep breathing, exercise, art, and journaling are valuable for helping your child cope with stress during this stage too. Engaging in puzzles and games that challenge their cognitive abilities also boosts critical-thinking and problem-solving skills.

Role-playing and talking about real-life situations where your child can apply the skills you're teaching can help them overcome everyday obstacles using safe solutions. Collaborating with your child also enables them to apply critical thinking to these situations and learn how to work with others.

However, you must find the balance between letting your child explore the world and their identity while still providing emotional support to prepare them for difficulties and ensure their well-being.

Adolescents and Teenagers Aged 13 to 15 Years Old

At this stage of development, your child is starting to explore their identity while also dealing with hormonal and emotional changes resulting from puberty. While it can be difficult to foster your child's exploration of their identity when your ex-partner has narcissistic tendencies, offering guidance and support will be important—especially since your child might explore a new identity every week. But no matter what your child says, they still need your guidance and love. Inviting extended family members into your child's life and seeking support from them can also benefit both of you during this stage.

Open and honest communication about the social, emotional, and physical changes your child is going through will be crucial and allow you to give your child reassurance and support. You also need to set clear rules and expectations for your child in your home. This is crucial when your ex-partner doesn't, or refuses to, do the same in their home.

Be sure to communicate openly with your child and remind them that as they gain more freedom with age, they also gain more responsibility. Discuss how your child's social life will start to shift, and ensure they understand how to practice safety and enforce boundaries in friendships and romantic relationships. Additionally, continuing to teach your child valuable life skills like cooking, cleaning, and time management is crucial.

Encourage your child to continue making connections outside the family too. This could look like joining sports or art groups or joining a youth spiritual group where they can meet people around their age.

Your child may also begin to openly express their feelings about your family's current situation as they get older. Help them understand that it's okay to have mixed emotions. If your child is showing signs of emotional distress, consider getting them professional help, like counseling, where they'll gain additional strategies and skills for coping.

Teenagers Aged 16 to 18 Years Old

Your teenager will start informing you how they'd prefer to spend their time with you and your ex-partner once they reach this stage. If their suggestions are safe and both you and your ex-partner agree, support your teenager's choices. Offering guidance and advice, even as they grow older, can benefit your teenager's mental and emotional well-being.

Encouraging them to take on new responsibilities, like getting a part-time job after school, can also boost your teenager's confidence. This can help them become more independent, as having extra money and time away from home gives them more freedom.

Their romantic relationships may become more important too. Ensure that you talk about boundaries and safety with your teenager, be honest with them, and let them have a say to ensure they follow the agreed-upon rules and make safe decisions.

Since this stage also involves making big decisions about your teenager's future, involve them in these choices. Let your child pick colleges, plan their career, and help them understand how finances affect these decisions. This empowers your teenager and lets them play an active role in shaping their future.

Now is also a good time to motivate your teenager to set and work toward personal goals. Support your child by offering guidance, helping them create action plans, and checking in on their progress. This can help your teenager feel accomplished and learn to take responsibility for their actions and choices.

However, your child might still make mistakes. Your presence in their life means the consequences of these mistakes should be within safe limits. This helps your teenager take accountability and understand the importance of making careful decisions. That's why it's important to continue developing your teenager's problem-solving and critical-thinking skills regardless of their age.

Simply talking about the possible outcomes of decisions and exploring different solutions are ways to continue this process. You should also set aside regular quality time for your teenager. This ensures your bond with your teenager remains strong and helps you notice possible problems, like signs of emotional distress.

Emotional Indicators of Distress

Children can't always name their emotions and may not even realize they're in distress, but their external behaviors can help us determine if something is wrong. Signs of emotional distress differ depending on the age of your child, but they're often considered any behavior your child doesn't normally display or exhibit to a severe degree. For example, when they become easily irritated when you interrupt them during homework time when they're normally calm. Other possible signs include

- changes in sleeping and eating patterns
- moodiness and irritability
- becoming overly clingy
- poor concentration and struggles at school they never had before
- routinely expressing worry
- showing fearful reactions
- withdrawing from social interactions
- crying, mood swings, and other behavioral changes
- complaining about school
- tummy aches or saying they feel sick

As every child is unique, you may struggle to be certain about whether your child is experiencing distress. Seeking additional guidance from a counselor, psychologist, or other mental health professional can be extremely valuable. They can also help you identify possible abuse by your ex-partner.

Strategies for Helping Your Child Manage Emotions

You could use several techniques to help your child manage their emotions. If you seek support from a counselor, for example, they may offer additional methods specifically tailored to your child and their unique circumstances. You can use the following strategies to help you get started:

- **Start as soon as possible.** From the moment your child is born, you can begin talking about emotions. Pointing out what characters are feeling when reading books together or watching a movie is just one great way to help your child learn how to identify emotions.

- **Teach your child to recognize their emotions and name them.** Once your child has calmed down after a meltdown, you could sit with them and calmly talk about how they felt when they had their meltdown. This includes helping them figure out why they may have felt that way and walking them through options of what they can do when they experience the same emotion next time. The key is to be patient and calm and talk when your child is in a calm headspace.

- **Model the behavior you want to see in your child.** Children learn a lot from watching their parents. If you know your ex-partner won't be a good role model for emotions, your child will need to learn to identify and manage emotions appropriately from you.

- **Continue building and maintaining a strong and trusting relationship with your child.** This will help them regulate their emotions better and develop a secure sense of attachment that will benefit them as they get older.

If your child has extended family that will be included in the co-parenting journey, teach them the strategies you're using so that your child is consistently reminded how to identify and manage their emotions regardless of who they are with. This can be more easily achieved when your child feels safe.

Creating a Safe Home Environment

This is the first step to fostering open and honest communication with your child. If your home, and the homes of extended family, provide your child with a sense of safety and comfort, they're more likely to open up about their feelings and talk about what's going on in their life. If they have a problem, they'll also feel more comfortable coming to you for help.

The following list provides you with the common factors involved in creating a safe home environment. In general, it's a space free from mental, emotional, and physical harm, but it's also more than catering to your child's basic needs.

- Avoid yelling and raising voices, as this can scare your child and make them feel like they're at fault even if you aren't yelling at them. If your child has made you angry, use calming techniques that help you talk with and discipline your child using an even tone of voice.

- Use daily routines to establish consistency and stability. Include bonding time with your child where you can play, read, or watch a movie together.

- Check in with your child throughout the day and set aside a specific time to talk about emotions.

- Let your child be a child in your home. Allow them time to hang out on their own, but also spend time with your child.

- To ensure your child follows the rules, respects boundaries, and accepts the consequences of their actions at any age, they'll need to understand your reason for putting these rules in place. Practice open and honest communication and allow your child to ask questions even if you won't change a fair rule.

- When your child tells you something, believe them. They may not be able to fully express themselves, but knowing that you will believe them ensures they come to you for help without fear of judgment or repercussions.

- Ensure that extended family members consistently implement the rules and boundaries you've established. Be sure to also communicate new rules, expectations, and how to approach problems so that your child experiences fair and consistent treatment no matter where they're staying.

- Allowing your child time with extended family is a great way to help them feel like they matter. This is also valuable for helping them connect to their cultural heritage and spiritual identity, emphasizing feelings of stability and belonging.

You could go one step further and design a physical space in the home that acts as a safe space.

Tips for Creating a Safe Space

This space should be placed away from loud noises or heavy traffic areas. Additionally, you can use the following tips to make the space inviting:

- Make the space cozy by adding soft furniture, pillows, blankets, or a beanbag.

- Add items with soft colors and different textures.

- If your child is very young, this space should only be used with supervision. As they get older, you can frequently check in on them to make sure they're okay.

- Remove any potential hazards from the space.

- Hang curtains or add a foldable screen that provides additional privacy.

- Include age-appropriate books, soft toys, and other toys that provide your child with comfort.

You could also designate this space as the zone where your child can share their emotions and feelings without judgment or fear of consequences. That way, if your child does need to ask for help but is afraid, they'll talk to you in this space without fear.

Journaling for Children

Encouraging your child to express their emotions using different methods is important. Since journaling is an effective strategy regardless of a person's age, you can provide your child with another safe space to vent, talk through problems, and identify feelings.

1. Begin by taking your child to the store and allowing them to pick out a journal they like. You could even purchase a journal designed for children that's age-appropriate.

2. Sit down with your child to explain how journaling works.

    A. Remind them that they don't need to worry about grammar and spelling in their journal, as no one but them will read it.

3. Create a list of prompts, like the ones below, that your child can use to guide their journaling activities:

   A. If the emotion you're feeling right now was a color, what color would it be?

   B. Describe what happiness feels like to you.

   C. Remember a moment when you felt very angry or sad. Describe what happened and explain why you were upset.

   D. Name three things that made you smile today.

   E. Describe your perfect friend.

The only way to effectively meet your child's needs when co-parenting is to understand what they are. While these needs will change as they get older, this understanding makes it easier to adjust your co-parenting approach. But since co-parenting involves your child traveling between different households, how do you help them cope with transitions?

Chapter 9:
Transitioning Your Child Between Homes

Transition smart, transition strong. Your kids deserve nothing less. –Di Stock

Traveling between your home and their other parent's home is one of the biggest transitions your child will face on the co-parenting journey. And in the beginning, it can be scary for you and your child. You both have to get used to being apart for certain periods and using other forms of contact, like video messaging, to communicate when you're apart. While this transition will happen frequently, it can still be difficult for children of any age. Luckily, there are several strategies you can use to make transitions easier.

Navigating Transitions

Moving between two homes can be difficult when the parent of one home, your ex-partner, has narcissistic tendencies. This may cause you to feel anxious and worry about your ex-partner's behavior around your child. You may also feel scared and lonely at first. For your child, being separated from you and being in a new space can be challenging too.

One of the key tips to success is to understand that transitions are challenging for you and your child and to give your child space, regardless of their age, after every transition so that they can settle in again.

Recognizing that even the easier transitions can be exhausting and overwhelming for you and your child helps you practice compassion, understanding, and patience with yourself and your child. Using additional tools, like the ones discussed in this section, will also help you create a consistent and balanced approach to this process that helps your child feel secure throughout the transition.

- **Use neutral drop-off locations:** A neutral drop-off location makes it easier to remain calm when your child is transitioning to their second home. Locations like schools and daycare centers are a great option since they minimize the amount of contact you have with your ex-partner, lowering the chances that your child picks up any tension. These structured environments can also make the transition process easier on your child by lowering their stress levels and ensuring they feel safe.

- **Allow time for your child to adjust:** After your child arrives, give them a few hours to settle back in and decompress after the transition. This could look like picking your child up after school on a Friday and giving them the evening to settle. You could still plan to eat dinner together and if your child doesn't want to talk yet, allow them to eat with minimal conversation. You can always talk tomorrow when they feel relaxed and comfortable again.

- **Acknowledge your child's emotions:** If your child finds transitioning between homes challenging or frustrating, allow them to express this. This includes listening when they ask to have a few hours of minimal interaction before catching up with you. Validating your child's emotions about the transition without judgment will encourage them to come to you to ask for help, support, or your company depending on what they need.

- **Maintain a consistent routine:** This has been repeated several times, but routines do provide a sense of safety, support, and comfort that will be invaluable during the transition process. Knowing what to expect when your child arrives can make it easier for them to cope and readjust when moving between the two homes.

- **Create a welcoming environment:** It's a good idea for your child to have two of everything, like hygiene products and familiar items like toys, books, and personal belongings so that there's little to no packing required when they transition between both homes. This also makes them feel more welcome in both homes. Allowing your child to make their bedroom their own in both homes also provides them with privacy for moments when they'd like to be alone.

- **Plan quality time with your child:** While your child should be allowed to have their alone time (depending on their age and the need for constant supervision), it can be beneficial to specifically set aside time to give your child your full attention. During this time, you can talk, read together, go out for an activity, or do something you both enjoy at home. This way, you strengthen your bond with your child and help them feel like they are a priority.

- **Gradually reintroduce responsibilities:** Age-appropriate responsibilities like homework and chores should be gradually reintroduced after your child arrives. So don't ask them to pack the dishes away five minutes after they've arrived. Instead, you could ask them to help you clear the table after dinner later that evening. This prevents your child from becoming overwhelmed.

- **Keep the communication channels open:** Open and honest communication will be crucial for ensuring your child asks for help when they need it. When you listen without judgment and make your child feel heard, they'll talk about their experiences, emotions, and problems, and ask questions. This is valuable for identifying potential issues arising as a result of your ex-partner's narcissistic tendencies. Communication also means keeping your child updated about changes in routines and plans, informing them about upcoming appointments and events, and when they will be visiting their other parent.

- **Reassure them:** Frequent reassurance and letting your child know that your home is a safe space can help them feel supported and cared for. But reassurance is also supported by ensuring consistency in routines and reinforcing rules and boundaries.

- **Plan transition activities:** They often consist of preparation and settling-in activities. For example, settling in could involve having a specific meal with your child when they arrive. The goal is to decrease the anxiety your child may feel during the transition and make it fun for both of you.

- **Monitor your child's behavior:** While your child may seem to handle the transition without issue, it's important to continue monitoring their behavior, as they may not always be able to verbalize that something is wrong or that they feel overwhelmed. Besides communicating with your child about what they may need, you can also use their behavior to adjust how you approach meeting their needs and the routines you follow.

The Role of Extended Family

Your child won't just be moving between your and your ex-partner's homes. They'll also travel to their aunts', uncles', and grandparents' houses. The strategies you'll use during these transitions won't change much but should be adapted according to the home your child is traveling to and their age.

Keeping a consistent routine but adding special traditions when visiting extended family is one way to help your child look forward to these visits. A tradition could be your children accompanying a family member to the mall and going for lunch or to the bookstore.

Open and honest communication with extended family members will also be vital. Ensure they know what the rules are, how to enforce boundaries, and what to do if your child misbehaves. This way, you can ensure consistent strategies and routines are being practiced regardless of the home your child is living in. It also provides your child with a sense of comfort due to this consistency.

But how do you ensure consistent discipline in a way that meets your parenting style?

Maintaining Discipline Across Households

In addition to co-parenting, you're also practicing a parenting style that you're comfortable with and fits your family's needs and values. This means you may have a specific way to approach misbehavior, like allowing your child to experience the natural consequences of their actions and talking about what happened.

Positive parenting is a great practice for co-parents since it helps you ensure consistent discipline that contributes toward stability and support for your child as they get older. Something that's important when your child transitions between homes where one parent has narcissistic tendencies.

This style of parenting is also great for implementing into your own parenting practices since it promotes behaviors meant to foster healthy and positive development. It's also based on principles related to teaching, leading, consistency, open communication, nurturing behaviors, affection, unconditional love, and prioritizing your child's best interests. This is especially important for children who have a parent with narcissistic tendencies. So, how can you practice this parenting style?

Tips for Positive Parenting

- **Use positive reinforcement.** It can be beneficial to catch your child being good and following the rules, and then recognizing and praising them for it. This reinforces the behavior and encourages them to repeat it. Hugs, compliments, and love are just a few simple ways to positively reinforce your child's behavior.

- **Show that your love is unconditional.** While you need to guide your child, ensure that the methods you use are nurturing and encouraging. This also helps your child understand that you will love them regardless of their behavior.

- **Practice clear and calm communication.** Children are more likely to follow the rules and accept the consequences of their actions when they understand why a rule is in place and what they did wrong. This helps them understand your expectations and gives your child an opportunity to offer input when there is a problem.

- **Ensure discipline is always fair and firm.** If you, your ex-partner, or extended family members say "no," you have to follow through and be firm. This applies to all the rules and boundaries you set, as it helps your child understand that you mean what you say.

- **Be consistent.** Any rules or boundaries that need to be followed in your home must also be followed in your ex-partner's and extended family member's home. This also supports the previous tip of fair and firm discipline, as it helps your child understand what to expect in each home and establishes a sense of security and stability.

- **Practice empathy and understanding.** Your child hasn't been in this world as long as you have. This means that things that may be easy and simple for you are actually quite scary and challenging for your child. So, be patient, try to stay calm (use calming techniques from previous chapters), and show your child empathy.

To ensure your parenting style is effective, you need to ensure that the strategies you use, methods of discipline, and other parenting activities are consistent in both homes, including the homes of extended family members. This means communicating effectively with your ex-partner and laying out the strategies and methods in your parenting plan so that you can ensure your child's safety when they aren't in your custody.

Keep in mind, however, that this isn't always possible, as it can be challenging to have this conversation depending on your ex-partner's narcissistic behaviors. If you cannot have this conversation, practice your chosen parenting style consistently in your home. That way, your child will have at least one stable home environment where they can thrive.

Action Steps

Transitions are a common part of everyday life. They can be as simple as your child moving from your home to the car to school, or even moving from reading a book with your child to helping them with their homework. This chapter has several strategies for helping your child transition between homes, but how do you help them move between activities?

The following exercise will help you develop a transition routine for daily activities so that the process can be more enjoyable for you and your child.

1. Start by listing the transitions you and your child will need to prepare for. For example, preparing to visit their other parent, getting ready for school or bed, or moving from playtime to doing their chores.

2. Choose one transition from your list and decide how you can make it fun.

    A. Use a visual timer that counts down how long your child has before they need to start the next activity.

B. Create a silly song that starts the transition process and ends as your child moves into the next activity.

C. Assign a specific activity that acts as the transition between two other activities. For example, a 2-minute meditation, 10 minutes of dancing to their favorite music, or having a snack break.

3. Use a blank poster board or page you and your child can see as you move around your home to set out the transition routines for common everyday activities.

Transitions are an important part of our lives. Knowing how to navigate them effectively can be crucial to your child coping with transitions in the future. This is where developing your child's resilience, using the strategies in the next chapter, can be beneficial to overcoming life's challenges.

Chapter 10:
Helping Your Child Build Resilience

Resilient kids aren't born—they're built by determined parents. –Di Stock

Resilience is a crucial skill for helping your child navigate living in two homes where one parent has narcissistic tendencies. By developing this trait, your child will have the skills needed to cope with uncertainty and change throughout their lives. This process of developing resilience begins with communicating with your child about the divorce or separation.

Helping Your Child Cope With Separation and Divorce

For children, the separation of their parents can feel like their whole world has been turned upside down, and you may even feel the same way. Besides remaining patient, providing reassurance, and listening to your child during this transition period, it's important to talk about the separation or divorce with them too. Communicating honestly helps your child understand that the separation is not their fault and that you and their other parent will still be a part of their life—even if life looks different now.

Talking About Divorce

It's up to you to decide what you share with your child about the divorce or separation, as no parent will experience the same circumstances. Start by considering the impact of what you share with your child about the divorce or separation to guide you in how you communicate these details. You can use the following points to guide you during this process:

- Your child's age can act as a guide for what details you share with them. Younger children, for example, need a simpler explanation compared to older children.

- If possible, first discuss with your ex-partner what you will share with your child and how you will explain it.

- Be honest during this conversation but avoid criticizing your ex-partner. This can be challenging when the split arises due to their narcissistic tendencies, but the goal is to put your child's best interests first.

- Reassure your child that you still love them and will be a part of their life, even if they'll be splitting their time between your home and their other parent's home.

- Share information related to changes in your child's living arrangements, routines, school, and other activities. Again, adjust the amount of detail given at first to prevent your child from becoming overwhelmed.

- Allow your child to ask questions and answer them as best as you can.

- Any changes to your child's life, like new living arrangements, should be planned before talking with your child to prevent uncertainty from making this already scary process more challenging.

The strategies for coping with transitions in the previous chapter will also be crucial during this conversation. Routines, comfort items, and purposefully spending time with your child are all strategies for making the divorce or separation easier too.

Supporting Your Child

Directly communicating with your child about the separation or divorce is great for preparing them for the changes that will come. You can use the following strategies to guide you in supporting your child:

- Look at the situation from your child's perspective. Recognize that while their experience may differ from yours, their feelings are still valid. This also helps you understand the changes in your child's behavior, like anger, sadness, and frustration.

- Encourage your child to feel these emotions so that they don't feel like they need to hide them. This could include avoiding phrases that imply the separation is best for everyone because even if that is the truth, your child may not feel the same.

- While family routines need to be adjusted to better suit the circumstances, it's important to keep practicing them. This includes family mealtimes, game nights, and attending events (like birthday parties) together. Your child needs to be reminded that while life is changing, your love and support are still unconditional.

- Unless there are safety concerns, encourage your child to maintain their relationship with their other parent and extended family members. This can support their mental and emotional well-being and offer support and stability during this transition.

- It takes time to figure out what works best according to your co-parenting situation. Talking about both sides of the family, offering connections between both homes (like keeping comfort items with them), and prioritizing your child's needs can make this process less uncertain.

Now that you have a starting point for developing resilience in your child, you can build on it. We'll do this by looking at emotional resilience for children.

Encouraging Emotional Expression

The ability to recover quickly and healthily from setbacks, difficulties, and adversities means knowing how to react to and cope with emotional and mental stress. This is a skill that can be beneficial for children of any age—but especially when they're in contact with their parent who has narcissistic tendencies.

Resilience is also crucial for helping children cope with and overcome the challenges arising from divorce, like living in two homes and school stressors like exams, peer pressure, and friendship rivalry. This trait helps children overcome life's challenges in a way that benefits their mental and emotional health instead of damaging it. But how do you know if your child is resilient or not?

Signs of Resilience in Children

When your child starts to develop resilience, you'll notice the following signs:

- An interest and enthusiasm for schoolwork and related activities.

- The ability to ask for help when they need it.

- Solving small problems on their own.

- Seeking out opportunities to practice responsibility.

- Demonstrating understanding and empathy toward others.

- Finding the good in situations and seeing them as an opportunity to improve their results.

- Understanding that their actions will cause a specific result.

Developing Your Child's Resilience

It's possible to help your child develop their resilience at any age. You'll also find it helpful to include extended family in this process. Having your child's grandparents, aunts, and uncles recognize their achievements, help them celebrate victories, and work with them to further develop their problem-solving skills builds your child's confidence. They also learn that the skills they work on with you can be practiced in various situations. In this section, you'll find a few strategies for helping your child develop emotional resilience.

Help Your Child Recognize Their Emotions

Regardless of your child's age, it can be valuable to sit with them during moments when they're struggling to help them acknowledge their emotions. This includes helping them label the emotion so they can work through it using activities like journaling, talking, movement, or play.

See Mistakes as Opportunities

Teaching your child to embrace their mistakes and see them as opportunities to grow and develop prevents them from fearing failure. This helps your child feel more confident about learning new skills and taking safe risks, allowing them to develop a growth mindset that encourages them to continue learning as they get older.

Teach Problem-Solving Skills

Your child will benefit more from being taught *how* to think than being taught *what* to think. This is done by giving your child opportunities to practice thinking about a problem. For example, role-playing problem scenarios offer your child the opportunity to identify and practice different solutions.

Model Adaptability

Since children learn by watching their parents, you can use this to your advantage. When you're faced with difficult situations where you struggle to manage your emotions, demonstrate how to stay calm. This could include apologizing to your child if you did unintentionally raise your voice. When you make mistakes, admit it so that your child also learns that mistakes are a natural part of life.

Additionally, resilience in children is strengthened by developing and nurturing their confidence in their abilities.

Building Self-Esteem and Confidence

Self-esteem and confidence are important contributors to a child's resilience and mental and emotional well-being. When well-developed, these traits can aid your child in their academics, social and familial relationships, and goal achievements now and in the future. In this section, you'll find two activities to help you develop these traits in your child.

Strength Journaling

This activity aims to help your child understand the importance of being themselves by recognizing what makes them unique.

1. In your child's journal, have them turn to a new page.

2. Divide the page into two columns.

3. Ask your child to list the things that make them who they are in the first column. For example, they might be loved by all animals or show kindness to everyone.

4. In the second column, have your child list everything they like about themselves.

5. Reflect through the two lists with your child and help them identify and write down their strengths.

Creating Personal Affirmations

Affirmations are valuable and work on the idea that the more you repeat a positive statement, the more likely you are to believe it. This is beneficial for helping your child develop a positive belief in their abilities. You can use the following guidelines to help your child create a set of meaningful personal affirmations:

1. Use the previous activity to help your child create a list of three to five positive statements. (Statements should be no longer than one sentence.)

2. Rewrite these statements onto small cards and allow your child to decorate them.

3. These cards can be carried by your child or placed in areas of the home where your child will frequently see them.

Your toolbox is now filled with everything you need to become a resilient co-parent and build a happy and healthy life for your child. Now it's time to shift the focus to your mental and emotional well-being.

Part 4:

Healing and Personal Growth

Through healing, find your strength. Through growth, find your purpose. –Di Stock

Chapter 11:
Learning to Prioritize Yourself

Don't just move on, move forward. Process your emotions and thrive. –Di Stock

After constantly putting the needs and wants of your ex-partner first for so long, it can be incredibly challenging to intentionally take care of yourself. Feelings of guilt and shame may arise as you aren't used to doing things that make you happy. That's why one of the biggest aspects of healing is making time for self-care and prioritizing your needs. And by focusing on your well-being, you'll be able to show up for your child and yourself in everyday life. The first step in this process is to reflect on the past.

Understanding Your Past to Build a Better Future

In previous chapters, you learned about narcissism and how it can manifest in relationships. This information provided insight into the narcissistic relationship cycle and the tactics your ex-partner may have used to stay in control. While you can't live in the past, you can learn from it to prevent it from repeating.

You've already begun implementing what you've learned from your relationship to build and enforce your boundaries, choose effective methods of communication, and redefine your relationship with your ex-partner. Now it's time to start moving forward so that you can rebuild your life and find your identity separate from your ex-partner.

Tips for Success

The following list contains helpful guidelines that you can use to assist you as you work through this chapter:

- **Understand that you're not at fault:** Your ex-partner hurting you, your child, and the other people in your life is their choice.

While you may feel confused, guilty, or ashamed during the healing journey, take a deep breath and remind yourself that you're not responsible for the actions and behaviors of others and they do not reflect your worth.

- **Shift the focus back to you:** After focusing solely on your ex-partner and their needs, you deserve to intentionally focus on yourself. During co-parenting, this looks like setting aside time for self-care. You also teach your child that it's important to prioritize self-care so that you can show up fully in the other areas of your life.

- **Rebuild your boundaries:** Again, boundaries are vital to helping you protect yourself against your ex-partner during the co-parenting journey. It also helps you ensure that your new life is protected against their narcissistic tendencies.

- **Filter things in your life:** Identify what does and doesn't work for you as you rebuild your life. Reassess old habits, relationship patterns, and thought patterns and decide whether they add value to your life. From there, you can either make adjustments or establish new habits, boundaries, and thought patterns that better serve your vision for your and your child's future.

- **Rebuild your trust in yourself:** Learning to trust yourself and your instincts after a relationship with a narcissist can be challenging, but it's also important. When you reflect on your relationship with your ex-partner, recognize and acknowledge the moments where your intuition was correct despite your ex-partner making you believe otherwise. This reinforces that you can trust your instincts.

- **Be patient with yourself:** Recovering from your relationship with your ex-partner and processing the trauma you've experienced isn't something that happens overnight or in a month. It takes time. Be sure to acknowledge and celebrate your success as well—no matter how small your victories may be at first.

- **Rely on your support system:** You now know how important your support network can be to your co-parenting journey. This system is also essential to offering you connection, emotional support, and a sense of belonging as you move forward with your life.

- **Seek professional help:** There is no shame in asking for help. Working with a counselor or a therapist can help you work on specific aspects of healing, like processing the specific trauma you experienced and learning how to trust other people again. Professionals can also provide guidance, insight, and support that can further benefit the healing work you're already doing by yourself.

Rebuilding your life is an opportunity for you to reinvent yourself. While you may only want to focus on your child, making time for healing will benefit your parenting abilities and your child. This means taking action.

To Get Different, We Must Do Different

The hurt your ex-partner has inflicted may overshadow any of the good times you had together. This doesn't mean you don't have good memories of your family, but it can make ending the relationship and moving forward difficult. That's why grieving your ex-partner and the loss of the relationship is crucial to healing.

Grieving a Relationship

Reacting to the loss of your relationship and ex-partner is natural. There's no shame in being upset, anxious, or scared. Such emotions are normal when you experience a drastic change in your life, regardless of the harm caused by your ex-partner.

By allowing yourself to grieve your relationship—even if you were the one to end it—you can process the emotions and trauma you've experienced. Grieving your relationship can also lower your risk of falling back into a relationship with your ex-partner, benefitting your co-parenting relationship. So, how does this process work?

Accept the Reality of the Breakup, Divorce, or Separation

Coming to terms with the end of your relationship with your ex-partner is vital to healing and a successful co-parenting relationship. It helps you break free from your past while recognizing that you've also experienced a great loss, and it's okay to be upset about it.

Thinking of your relationship in the past tense helps you redefine your relationship with your ex-partner. It's easier to become unstuck from your past so that you can begin looking toward your future too. So, acknowledge the loss and its impact so that you can take the first step toward healing.

Allow Yourself to Feel Your Emotions

Experiencing various emotions around your separation or divorce, often felt to an intense degree, is normal during the grieving process. Anger, loneliness, sadness, shame, guilt, despair, pain, happiness, anxiety, and overwhelm are only a few of the emotions you may experience.

What's important is that you don't avoid your emotions or deny them. Regardless of their intensity, feeling your emotions without judging yourself for them is crucial to understanding them. Talking about your emotions with someone you trust, journaling, meditating, or exercising are examples of how you can process these emotions, helping you to work through them in a way that meets your needs.

Tips for Processing Emotions

We all process our emotions in different ways. While it can be valuable to work with a professional, you can also make use of the following tips:

- **Don't fight your feelings:** Negative and positive emotions are a normal part of life. While their intensity can be overwhelming when you've been hurt by your past relationship, acknowledging and feeling these emotions helps you understand them and yourself better. Moving forward with your life also becomes easier when your emotions aren't holding you back.

- **Understand that emotions aren't permanent:** You won't be experiencing the pain of loss or anger at your ex-partner for the rest of your life, or at least not to the intensity you're currently experiencing these feelings. Remember that as you heal, joy, calm, and contentment are emotions you will experience again.

- **Talk with someone you trust:** They could be a friend, family member, or a professional like a counselor or therapist. Having an outside perspective can give you insight into the origins of your emotions and how to process them. Venting to another person can also be a very therapeutic activity.

- **Focus on taking care of yourself on purpose.** Make time for self-care so that you can purposefully care for your mental, emotional, and physical well-being. This includes eating well, getting enough sleep, exercising, journaling, meditating, and making time for the things you enjoy.

Start Taking Steps to Adjust to the Change

Your life will undergo several big changes once you've left your ex-partner. New childcare arrangements, living space, daily routines, and financial worries are just a few examples. You may even have to figure out who you are as an individual without your ex-partner trying to shape you into someone else.

This stage can be very scary, but it's also crucial to your journey of healing and growth. Many of the strategies you need to succeed during this stage can be found in previous chapters, including establishing new boundaries, building a strong relationship with your child, and turning your home into a safe space.

Rebuild Your Life

This stage builds on the previous step. By taking action, you start the process of rebuilding your life. While your new life will be unique to you and your child, as well as your situation, you can embrace this change. It can take time to accomplish, but you'll start noticing that even the smallest changes contribute to your goals for your future. This includes spending time with your child, cherishing happy memories, and acknowledging your past without getting stuck.

Life doesn't stop when you leave your ex-partner. However, it's up to you to decide what your future will look like. It may even include your extended family if you get along well with them. Reconnecting with your parents, grandparents, friends, siblings, aunts, and uncles provides you with connection, a sense of belonging, stability, and support during this tumultuous time. If you need help or support, reach out to them.

Practicing Self-Compassion

Being compassionate toward yourself and your current situation is about showing yourself love, forgiveness, patience, and acceptance. Showing yourself compassion during your healing journey allows you to nurture yourself without judgment. It's also valuable for your growth as an individual since you recognize that you're more than a parent and more than what your ex-partner tried to shape you into. The following principles define self-compassion:

- **Self-kindness:** Your ability to show yourself understanding and kindness without judging or criticizing yourself for your mistakes, lapses in judgment, or the challenges you've faced.

- **Mindfulness:** Being aware of your emotions, thoughts, interactions with the world, and sensory experiences in the present moment. This helps you develop an awareness of yourself and the world without becoming lost in the past or potential future.

- **Common humanity:** This principle is about recognizing that, unfortunately, suffering occurs all over the world. You're not alone in your struggles, and you can acknowledge this and use it to connect with other parents going through similar experiences. This helps you build a community and experience life alongside these individuals.

But what are some of the ways that you can show yourself compassion?

Self-Compassion Techniques

There are several ways to practice this skill. The following list of activities provides you with a starting point:

- **Treat yourself as you would your friend.** Allow yourself to make mistakes without judgment or criticism. Be sure to take care of yourself by nurturing your mental and emotional well-being too.

- **Become more mindful.** Developing your self-awareness through this practice helps you get to know yourself better. You also gain insight into your behaviors during certain situations so that you can improve how you respond to them in the future.

- **Accept yourself as you are.** Recognize that while you can and should grow as a person, it's still okay to accept that you have flaws and weaknesses like everyone else. Accepting your flaws gives you the strength to heal and makes it easier to be kind to yourself.

Battling Negative Self-Talk

When your inner voice or the way you talk to yourself is critical, focuses on the negative, or makes you feel bad, you are practicing negative self-talk. It often arises as a result of your ex-partner's treatment of you and can cause further harm to your confidence and self-esteem, preventing you from working toward your goals, and causing you to believe that you will fail no matter what.

This could manifest as statements such as, "I'm not good enough." But just because the voice inside your head told you something doesn't mean it's true. Luckily, you can break this self-talk cycle using the following points as a guide:

- **Use mindfulness to become aware of what you tell yourself.** This allows you to identify negative thoughts without dwelling on them, but it also helps you amend your self-talk.

- **Write down your thoughts.** By writing your negative thoughts down, you can challenge them and determine if they're true. You may also find it easier to shift your thinking to an optimistic and realistic pattern when you can see your thoughts.

- **Be mindful of the content you consume.** Social media, the news, and the people you surround yourself with can affect your inner voice. Becoming more aware of what you consume and its impact on you can make it easier to combat negative self-talk.

Taking action to build a better future doesn't have to be complicated. You can take small steps. What truly matters is that you're trying to do better for yourself and your child.

Moving Forward

Healing from your past relationship means finding closure. While everyone processes trauma in their own time, this is an important step for moving forward. The problem is that finding closure with your ex-partner can be challenging because of their narcissistic tendencies. So, what can you do instead?

- **Create your closure within yourself.** This could involve writing a letter that you won't send that sets out your feelings, thoughts, opinions, and experiences during your relationship. This helps you release and let go of the emotions and energy you've been holding on to since separating from your ex-partner.

- **Grieve your relationship.** While you experienced a lot of hurt from your past relationship, there may still have been good moments and an emotional connection on your part that you need to grieve before you can move forward with your life.

- **Don't stay in the past.** You can't go back and change time, but you can decide to move forward and build a life with your child that makes you happy.

The techniques discussed throughout this chapter and book will help you move forward with your life and redefine your relationship with your ex-partner. But moving forward also means setting new goals.

Goal Setting

Goals can guide your growth and healing journey. This is helpful when you're figuring out who you are without your ex-partner. Everyone's goals will look different, but you can use the following guidelines to set new goals:

1. Write down your thoughts about what you want to achieve during the healing, growth, and co-parenting journey like you would a regular journal entry.

2. Reflecting on this entry, identify specific goals and list them on a new page.

3. Use the SMART principles that follow to help you refine the goals on your list:

   A. **Specific:** Specify what you would like to accomplish on your journey and detail the steps you'd have to take to achieve it.

   B. **Measurable:** Can you measure your progress? This could include creating a healthier routine and tracking your ability to consistently practice it.

   C. **Achievable:** Be realistic about what you can achieve right now and in the next few months. After all, you'll still have your regular responsibilities as a parent and adult while also adjusting to life post-divorce or separation.

   D. **Realistic:** Understand whether the goals you set are relevant to your growth and healing journey. While you can set additional goals for your career or hobbies, start small and focus on one set of goals to get started.

   E. **Timely:** Create a reasonable and achievable timeframe that prevents you from procrastinating.

4. Use a poster board to set your goals out in an easy-to-read manner.

5. Place this board in an area of your home where you will be constantly reminded of what you're working toward.

The healing journey looks different for everyone, but the work that you put in will be worth it. Don't delay. Start right now and work toward a healthier you, even if the first step you take is small.

Self-Reflection Journaling Challenge

Journaling is a great activity for reflecting on the past, gaining insight into your thoughts and emotions, and working out what you want from the future. The following prompts have been set out as a challenge. You will work on a prompt a day for seven days.

- **Day 1:** Describe the areas of your life that are currently causing you emotional pain.

- **Day 2:** Reflect on your relationship with your ex-partner and explain what emotions you experienced due to unmet needs.

- **Day 3:** Use images or metaphors to describe your emotions. Acknowledge these feelings and validate them without judgment.

- **Day 4:** Write a letter to your ex-partner (you won't send it) that describes your hurt, anger, and frustration during your relationship.

- **Day 5:** Explain what you believe is holding you back from living the life you want.

- **Day 6:** Observe your thoughts for a day and write down all the negative thoughts, opinions, and criticisms you had. Use the first list to reframe your thoughts so that they're more positive.

- **Day 7:** Use the previous day's statements to create your own list of personal and meaningful affirmations.

Now that you've begun your healing journey, you need to learn to take care of yourself. In the final chapter, we'll look at the strategies you can use to rediscover your true self and nurture them.

Chapter 12:
Rediscovering Yourself

In the journey of rebuilding your life, rediscover the extraordinary strength within you. This is not just a new chapter—it's the beginning of your greatest story yet. –
Di Stock

The truth is, you've changed. You're not the same person you were when you first entered into a relationship with your ex-partner because of the impact their narcissistic tendencies have had on you. You've experienced trauma, become a parent, and had to go through many challenges to get to this point in your life. Focusing on your healing journey gives you the opportunity to rediscover yourself and figure out who you want to be as an individual and a parent, but you have to embrace this new person and nurture them.

Finding Yourself After Divorce

Post-divorce or separation is a time for rediscovery. It's a process that begins as soon as you start the healing journey, but it can still be scary to realize that you're not the same person you once were. You're getting to know your new likes, dislikes, boundaries, and favorite hobbies. Things that have changed after being in a relationship with someone who is a narcissist.

This process takes time, but it's valuable for helping you get to know who you are outside the confines of your co-parenting relationship and role as a parent. This process of rediscovery doesn't happen overnight or by using a single activity. Although, you can use the core elements of this practice as a guide on this journey.

Key Principles of Rediscovery

Figuring out who you are post-divorce or separation may make you feel anxious. This journey does look different for everyone, but you can use the following principles to guide you on your unique path.

Embody Resilience and Inner Strength

Co-parenting with a narcissist is challenging, but use the challenge to help you develop your resilience. Allow yourself to reflect on your progress and successes, and celebrate your newfound strength and resilience. These traits will aid your journey of growth and help you endure and overcome challenges in the future.

Live Authentically and Boldly

Rediscovering yourself, your values, and your beliefs means embracing them. While you may have had to set them aside during your relationship with your ex-partner, it's time to live authentically. Take up space, work toward your dreams, and allow yourself to stand out.

Find Joy and Fulfillment

Life is a journey. Healing from the past and planning for the future are important, but you need to enjoy the present too. Find the small and big joys in everyday life, and pursue the activities and habits that make you happy and provide fulfillment. Find things that make you smile and laugh, spend time working on activities that bring you feelings of contentment, and embrace the people and situations that make you think, *Finally, I'm free to be me.*

These principles are great for guiding and aiding growth, but let's now take a look at some of the strategies that can support your journey of rediscovery.

Strategies That Aid Rediscovery

The healing journey creates the foundation for rediscovery. By accepting and understanding the experiences you've had and cultivating your self-awareness, you lay the groundwork for rediscovering your true self, your values, and your dreams. And as you begin healing, you'll gain the clarity and insight needed to find a new direction in life and nurture your authentic self. You have many strategies to choose from, however, the following tips can guide you as well:

- **Break free from labels:** Labels and expectations try to shrink us into boxes we often don't fit into. Instead, give yourself the freedom to explore who you are without judgment or shame.

- **Embrace your independence:** You no longer have to be held back by past relationships. Take charge and rediscover what you want from life and pursue it—even if this means doing it alone.

- **Refresh your wardrobe:** You probably neglected yourself during your relationship with your ex-partner. Take this time to refresh your wardrobe. Do your hair, get new clothes, take up new hobbies, and purposefully build a healthier life.

- **Practice self-reflection:** Take this time to reflect on your desires, beliefs, and values. They help you figure out what you want your life to look like and what goals will help you achieve this future.

No one can tell you who you are, what you like, or what you're worth. Only you can do this. Repeat these statements to yourself (or write them down and stick them on your mirror) as often as you can because your ex-partner won't want you to realize this as it diminishes their power over you.

And as scary and lonely as it can be, embrace your singleness and figure out who you really are before you seek out new romantic relationships. And don't let singleness or co-parenting stop you from pursuing the opportunities that arise during healing either.

Embrace New Opportunities in Your Life

Discovering who you are outside the confines of your relationship with your ex-partner and as a co-parent will create opportunities in different aspects of your life. You may decide that you'd like to make a change in your career, like learning a new skill or pursuing a beloved hobby in a professional capacity. Or perhaps you'd like to start dating again or expand your friendship circle.

You don't always have to say yes to new opportunities, but it's important to keep an open mind. You never know what you might learn or how it could benefit your life until you've taken the time to assess the opportunity.

It's difficult to provide specific guidelines around this process since new opportunities look different depending on your lifestyle, career path, and where you are on your journey. But you can use the guidelines in this section to navigate opportunities in the various areas of your life.

Your Personal Life

Divorce and separation allow you to reinvent yourself and rebuild your life—which we've discussed in Chapter 11 and the previous section. You also have a newfound sense of freedom and independence that will affect how you show up for yourself, your child, your career, and your friendships.

Take time to work on your relationships with friends and family too. They can be a crucial part of your support network. You also need to nurture your relationships with these individuals. This could include attending events like weekly coffee meetups or going to the movies. You could also go to family events like birthday parties or invite family over for dinner.

Your Career

After divorce or separation, set aside time to reflect on your new circumstances and how your career may be affected. Determine what you want from your professional life and start setting goals that will help you achieve them, like learning a new skill or applying for a promotion.

Setting realistic expectations, understanding that you're not alone, and celebrating your progress are small ways in which you can approach your professional life and build the career you've always dreamed of.

Your Romantic Life

You may decide to stay single for a while or actively pursue a romantic relationship later in your journey. Either way, navigating the dating world can be challenging. The most vital key to success is trusting your instincts and entering the dating world knowing who you are and what you're looking for in a relationship—don't settle for anything less.

Opportunities in your personal life arise because you no longer have to set aside your needs or wants to prioritize your narcissistic ex-partner. But it's up to you to take action and find fulfillment in the different areas of your life.

Rediscovery Bucket List

Figuring out what you enjoy doesn't have to be difficult. Use the guidelines that follow to help you start this process:

1. In your journal, list the activities or hobbies you've always enjoyed but may have stopped due to your ex-partner.

2. Add any activities you currently enjoy.

3. Create a second list of activities or hobbies you have always wanted to try but never had the time for.

4. Read through this list and circle the activities that appeal to you or that you would like to try again.

5. On a new page in your journal, write the heading "Rediscovery Bucket List."

6. Under this heading, add the activities you circled from the previous instructions.

7. Choose at least one activity a week, or as often as you can, to try out.

    A. Purposefully set aside time for this exercise.

    B. Ask your friends to join you for activities they may also be interested in.

8. Once you've tried an activity, note how you felt, if you'd like to do it again, or if it wasn't as enjoyable as it used to be.

Rediscovering your true self is a journey and while healing does take time and energy, it truly is worth the time and effort you put in. My hope is that you will take on the challenge and use the tools and strategies throughout this book to help you succeed and experience the joy that accompanies the journey of healing and growth. Now, all that's left to do is take action.

Conclusion

At this point in your journey, you're ready to become the resilient co-parent you envisioned when you first started this book. Resilience is a trait that benefits you in many areas of your life, but it's especially valuable for co-parenting with a narcissist.

Understanding what co-parenting is and how it works when your ex-partner has narcissistic tendencies allows you to decide if this parenting method is possible. Parallel parenting, for example, may be the better option for your family if your ex-partner is dangerous or co-parenting with them isn't possible.

Knowing what narcissism is and how it has manifested during your relationship helps you navigate these tendencies during co-parenting. This is helpful for redefining your relationship with your ex-partner after divorce or separation. You know what red flags to look out for and how your ex-partner might try to manipulate you into doing what they want. This information is also useful for your child to learn as their relationship with their other parent is redefined in the context of the divorce or separation.

Unfortunately, you may still face conflict during the co-parenting relationship. Your ex-partner's narcissistic traits can make it challenging for them to prioritize the needs of your child above their own. They may also disagree with decisions simply because they didn't make it. But you don't have to accept this.

Setting and reinforcing your and your child's boundaries, using various communication techniques, and seeking legal help in the form of mediators and parenting plans are just a few strategies that help you actively combat narcissistic tendencies without actively confronting or fighting with your ex-partner. This also helps you minimize your child's exposure to conflict.

Understanding how parental alienation may be used to destroy your relationship with your child gives you the means to fight back. In serious cases, you'll need the guidance of an experienced family lawyer. Fortunately, there are also many techniques—like the ones discussed in Chapter 5—that help you strengthen your bond with your child regardless of your ex-partner's use of manipulation tactics. This helps you nurture your and your child's mental and emotional well-being while protecting your relationship from serious damage.

Through the use of family-focused strategies, you can now create a safe, stable, supportive, and nurturing home environment that allows you and your child to flourish as well. This includes using transition strategies to make the move between homes smoother and building your child's resilience by boosting their confidence and self-esteem.

Getting the extended family involved is an important part of this journey too. They can offer support, connection, and a sense of belonging to you and your child during challenging times like divorce and separation. Their involvement also helps your child understand that while the family dynamic may be changing, they are still loved and cared for.

But you have to take time to focus on your own needs. Making time for self-care and healing from your relationship with your ex-partner is possible. This process is also crucial to helping you become the co-parent you've always envisioned. By embracing your authentic self and accepting that you have changed, you teach your child that their self-worth isn't dependent on anyone else. So, as guilty as you may feel when you take time for yourself at first, remember that the benefits and effort you put in are worth it.

Remember to refer to Appendix A too. There are several legal and financial resources you can use to aid your journey. It's also helpful to do your own research on child custody laws and support groups for victims of narcissistic abuse in your country and state.

Navigating co-parenting can be challenging, but you now have the tools you need to succeed. Your efforts and the time you put into this journey are a testament to your strength and dedication as both an individual and a parent. Every step you take, no matter how small, is a victory. So, keep moving forward and know that you are creating a more positive future for yourself and your children.

Your courage in facing the challenges of co-parenting and healing from a narcissistic relationship is admirable and deserves to be celebrated. Allow yourself to embrace the journey and know that your resilience will act as your guide to a better, healthier life for you and your child.

Appendix A:

Legal and Financial Resources

Resources Support Groups

In the following list, you will find the links you can use to access narcissistic abuse recovery support groups:

- Lists of international organizations and resources for victims of domestic violence and abuse:

    o **Shelters and programs in the US and Canada:** www.domesticshelters.org/help

    o **Shelters and programs outside the US and Canada:** www.domesticshelters.org/resources/national-global-organizations/international-organizations

- **National Domestic Violence Hotline:** www.thehotline.org

- **I Believe You:** www.ibelieveyourabuse.com/recovery

Legal Resources

In the following section, you'll find a variety of legal resources to guide you on your journey.

Legal Aid Resources

- Legal resources related to family law topics: americafamilylawcenter.org/topics/

- Help for finding an affordable lawyer:

    - **Talking Parents:** talkingparents.com/blog/what-if-i-cant-afford-a-lawyer

    - **Unbundled Legal Help:** family.unbundledlegalhelp.com/family-law/haverhill-ma

    - **Just Answer Child Support Legal Aid:** www.justanswer.com/sip/child-support-1?

- **Custody X Change:** The app offers additional guidance on all matters related to your rights and responsibilities as a parent; www.custodyxchange.com/signedup/portal.php

Parenting Plan Information

- Step-by-step guide on creating your custom parenting plan, including a template: www.custodyxchange.com/topics/software/parenting-plan-template.php

- Additional parenting plan information can be found here:

    - **Template LAB:** templatelab.com/parenting-plans/

    - **Legal Templates:** legaltemplates.net/form/parenting-plan/

    - **Custody X Change:** www.custodyxchange.com/topics/plans/overview/parenting-plan.php

Custody Arrangement Resources

Additional information on custody agreements, as well as templates:

- **Custody X Change:** www.custodyxchange.com/topics/plans/overview/custody-agreement-template.php

- **Coco Sign:** cocosign.com/agreement-template/custody/

Budgeting Templates

Budgeting templates that you can use to get started:

- **Canva:** www.canva.com/templates/s/budget/

- **Notion:** www.notion.so/templates/category/budgets

Financial Resources

In the following list, you'll find valuable videos for building your knowledge about finances and how you can pursue financial freedom post-divorce:

- **A Path to Financial Recovery After Divorce:** www.youtube.com/watch?v=g7gHqKDoPi0

- **The Creative Divorce:** www.youtube.com/watch?v=zZJnGwYPVCY&list=PLFv-j5IH9DXkU62vA_MOszzAu5oaRTKr_

- **Rebecca Zung:** www.youtube.com/watch?v=8K_EKUmGJyA

References

All the chapter opener quotes are the author's own words.

A Path to Financial Recovery After Divorce. (2022). *Post-divorce financial mistake: Not adjusting your lifestyle post-divorce—Mike Jurek, Esq.* [Video]. YouTube. https://www.youtube.com/watch?v=g7gHqKDoPi0

Admin. (2019, October 3). *William Worden's four tasks of grief.* The Therapy Centre. https://thetherapycentre.ie/william-wordens-four-tasks-of-grief/

Admin. (2023, February 17). A guide to extended family visitation rights. *Jones Divorce Law.* https://jonesdivorcelaw.com/blog/a-guide-to-extended-family-visitation-rights/

Adriane. (2019, January 8). *Routines for kids: Why they work & how to create your own.* Raising Kids with Purpose. https://raisingkidswithpurpose.com/routines-for-kids/

Affordable family law lawyer in Haverhill, MA. (2015). Unbundled Legal Help. https://family.unbundledlegalhelp.com/family-law/haverhill-ma

Arabi, S. (2017, August 21). *11 signs you're the victim of narcissistic abuse.* PsychCentral. https://psychcentral.com/blog/recovering-narcissist/2017/08/11-signs-youre-the-victim-of-narcissistic-abuse#1

Arnold, B. (2024, March 3). *How to spot an overt narcissist.* Overcomers Counseling. https://overcomewithus.com/narcissist-personality/how-to-spot-an-overt-narcissist

Arzt, N. (2023, May 9). *Co-parenting with a narcissist: 13 tips*. Choosing Therapy. https://www.choosingtherapy.com/co-parenting-with-narcissist/

Avoiding a loyalty conflict. (2023, March). Naître et grandir. https://naitreetgrandir.com/en/step/3-5-years/family-life/avoiding-loyalty-conflict/

BIFF: Quick responses to high conflict people, their personal attacks, hostile email and social media by Bill Eddy, LCSW Esq. (n.d.). Thompson Family Law. https://www.familylawfla.com/articles/biff-quick-responses-to-high-conflict-people-their-personal-attacks-hostile-email-and-social-media/

Bishop, S. (2023, June 4). *6 ways to stay calm and collected during a heated argument*. Mediate.com. https://mediate.com/6-ways-to-stay-calm-and-collected-during-a-heated-argument/

Boogaard, K. (2023, December 26). How to write SMART goals (with examples). *Work Life by Atlassian*. https://www.atlassian.com/blog/productivity/how-to-write-smart-goals

Bowen, D. (2022, October 1). *BIFF communication for co-parents after a divorce*. The Law Office of Deanna J. Bowen. https://www.deannabowen.com/biff-communication-for-coparents-after-a-divorce/

Breaking free: Embracing a fresh start after divorce. (2023, July 5). Guideway Legal Document and Mediation Services. https://guidewaylegal.com/breaking-free-embracing-a-fresh-start-after-divorce/

Budget templates. (2020). Canva. https://www.canva.com/templates/s/budget/

Budgets templates. (2024). Notion. https://www.notion.so/templates/category/budgets

Building a good relationship with your child. (2016, July 13). Positive Parenting Project. https://anitacleare.co.uk/building-a-good-relationship-with-your-child/

Building a support network and community. (2024). BC Children's Hospital Kelty Mental Health Resource Centre. https://keltymentalhealth.ca/building-a-support-network-and-community

The building blocks of self-compassion. (n.d.). My Best Self 101. https://www.mybestself101.org/building-blocks-of-selfcompassion

Burch, K. (2023, December 5). *5 signs of narcissistic abuse.* Verywell Health. https://www.verywellhealth.com/narcissistic-abuse-5220194

Charlie Health Editorial Team. (2023, September 1). *Things narcissists say in an argument (& what they really mean).* Charlie Health. https://www.charliehealth.com/post/things-narcissists-say-in-an-argument-and-what-they-really-mean#

Cherry, K. (2023, May 3). *How resilience helps you cope with challenges.* Verywell Mind. https://www.verywellmind.com/what-is-resilience-2795059

Child custody agreement template: Sole or joint custody. (2024). Custody X Change. https://www.custodyxchange.com/topics/plans/overview/custody-agreement-template.php

Child custody trials in New York: Tips for preparing. (2024). Custody X Change.

https://www.custodyxchange.com/locations/usa/new-york/trial.php

Child support legal aid. (2024). JustAnswer. https://www.justanswer.com/sip/child-support-1?

ChildPsych. (2021, December 12). *The importance of a support network for parents.* https://www.childpsych.co.za/the-importance-of-a-support-network-for-parents/

Chowdhury, M. R. (2019, January 22). *What is emotional resilience? (+6 proven ways to build it).* PositivePsychology.com. https://positivepsychology.com/emotional-resilience/#emotional-resilience

Co-parenting and joint custody tips for divorced parents. (2024, February 5). HelpGuide.org. https://www.helpguide.org/articles/parenting-family/co-parenting-tips-for-divorced-parents.htm

Conflict management when you're co-parenting. (2022, September 15). Raising Children Network. https://raisingchildren.net.au/grown-ups/family-diversity/co-parenting/conflict-former-partner

Copley, L. (2023, November 30). *30 best journaling prompts for improving mental health.* PositivePsychology.com. https://positivepsychology.com/journaling-prompts/#

Corelli, C. (2024, June 26). *Narcissistic abuse quiz—10 telltale signs you're dealing with a narcissist.* Carla Corelli. https://www.carlacorelli.com/quiz/narcissistic-abuse-quiz/

Cox, J. (2022, November 3). *How to recover from narcissistic abuse.* PsychCentral. https://psychcentral.com/disorders/narcissistic-personality-disorder/narcissistic-abuse-recovery-healing-from-the-discard#supporting-someone-else

Creating a safe & open home environment. (2016, May 3). *All for Kids.* https://www.all4kids.org/news/blog/creating-a-safe-open-home-environment/

Creating and using safe spaces. (2024, March 14). First Witness Child Advocacy Center. https://firstwitness.org/news/creating-and-using-safe-spaces/

The Creative Divorce. (2024). *Unlock financial confidence: Sunny's divorce recovery wisdom | Money With Sunny* [Video]. YouTube. https://www.youtube.com/watch?v=zZJnGwYPVCY

Cuncic, A. (2024, February 12). *7 active listening techniques for better communication.* Verywell Mind. https://www.verywellmind.com/what-is-active-listening-3024343

Custody agreement. (2022). Cocosign. https://cocosign.com/agreement-template/custody/

The Custody X Change app sign-up page. (n.d.). Custody X Change. https://www.custodyxchange.com/signedup/portal.php

Daino, J. E. (2022, February 4). How to set family boundaries: A therapist's guide. *Talkspace.* https://www.talkspace.com/blog/family-boundaries/

Daniel-Farrell, J. (2015, July 28). *Coping with divorce: The value of mindfulness practices.* Life Connections Counseling. https://lifeconnectionscounseling.com/coping-divorce-value-mindfulness-practices/

Davies, A. (2024, May 27). Benefits of mediation. *Mediator Academy.* https://www.mediatoracademy.com/blog/benefits-of-mediation

Design a parenting plan with our step-by-step template. (n.d.). Custody X Change.

https://www.custodyxchange.com/topics/software/parenting-plan-template.php

Divorce. (2024, February). YoungMinds. https://www.youngminds.org.uk/parent/parents-a-z-mental-health-guide/divorce/

Doll, K. (2019, March 23). *23 resilience building activities & exercises for adults.* PositivePsychology.com. https://positivepsychology.com/resilience-activities-exercises/#techniques

Dorwart, L. (2023, June 21). *7 types of narcissism.* Verywell Health. https://www.verywellhealth.com/narcissistic-personality-disorder-types-5213256

Dremen, A. (2020, September 21). *Writing reflections to heal from toxic relationships.* Medium. https://anescedremen.medium.com/writing-reflections-to-heal-from-toxic-relationships-f50b12272e2b

Duffy, R. (2023, March 11). *49 free parenting plan & custody agreement templates.* TemplateLab. https://templatelab.com/parenting-plans/

Eddy, B. (2019, May 15). *Who are high-conflict people?* High Conflict Institute. https://highconflictinstitute.com/high-conflict-strategies/who-are-high-conflict-people/

The Editors of Encyclopedia Britannica. (2024). Family court. In *Encyclopædia Britannica.* https://www.britannica.com/topic/family-court

The 8 principles of parenting for the 6-12 year-old child. (2021). Attachment Parenting International Nurturings. https://www.nurturings.org/6-12-child-principles

Encouraging positive behavior: Tips. (2024, June 7). Raising Children Network. https://raisingchildren.net.au/toddlers/behaviour/encouraging-good-behaviour/good-behaviour-tips

Episode 35—Co-parenting transitions: Do they ever get easier? (2023, February 14). Healthy Mom after Divorce. https://healthymomafterdivorce.com/episode-35-co-parenting-transitions-do-they-ever-get-easier/

Family routines: How and why they work. (2023, April 5). Raising Children Network. https://raisingchildren.net.au/grown-ups/family-life/routines-rituals-relationships/family-routines

Financial planning before, during, and after a divorce. (2023, July 28). SmartAsset. https://smartasset.com/financial-advisor/divorce-financial-planning

Find a shelter or program near you. (2024). DomesticShelters.org. https://www.domesticshelters.org/help#?page=1

4 play activities to help children manage emotions. (2023, December 19). HealthyChildren.org. https://www.healthychildren.org/English/family-life/power-of-play/Pages/play-ideas-to-help-your-child-manage-emotions.aspx

The 4 phases of the narcissist abuse cycle. (2022, December 17). Florida Women's Law Group. https://www.floridawomenslawgroup.com/the-4-phases-of-the-narcissist-abuse-cycle

4 ways to boost your self-compassion. (2021, February 12). Harvard Health Publishing. https://www.health.harvard.edu/mental-health/4-ways-to-boost-your-self-compassion

Free legal resource related to family law topics. (2022, February 23). America Family Law Center. https://americafamilylawcenter.org/topics/

Gallagher, J. (2021, November 3). *Co-parenting: Helping kids transition from one house to the other (and back again).* Divorce Ex. https://exexperts.com/mypost/co-parenting-helping-kids-transition-from-one-house-to-the-other/

Get professional help if you need it. (n.d.). Mental Health America. https://mhanational.org/get-professional-help-if-you-need-it

Gillette, H. (2023, November 25). *3 narcissistic traits in women.* PsychCentral. https://psychcentral.com/health/the-difference-between-male-and-female-narcissists

Gillette, H. (2023, January 27). *Recognizing the signs of coercive control.* PsychCentral. https://psychcentral.com/health/coercive-control

Gillis, K. (2022, November 10). *9 narcissistic manipulation tactics & how to deal.* Choosing Therapy. https://www.choosingtherapy.com/narcissistic-manipulation-tactics/

Gupta, S. (2024, May 15). *How to identify and escape a narcissistic abuse cycle.* Verywell Mind. https://www.verywellmind.com/narcissistic-abuse-cycle-stages-impact-and-coping-6363187

Hammond, C. (2019, August 16). *How to counteract parental alienation.* PsychCentral. https://psychcentral.com/pro/exhausted-woman/2019/08/how-to-counteract-parental-alienation#1

Hauck, C., Pal, P., Goldstein, E., Bobinet, K., & Bradley, C. (2018, August 27). *5 simple mindfulness practices for daily life.* Mindful. https://www.mindful.org/take-a-mindful-moment-5-simple-practices-for-daily-life/

Hawekotte, L. (2024, May 22). *The importance of a financial plan in divorce proceedings.* LinkedIn. https://www.linkedin.com/pulse/importance-financial-plan-divorce-proceedings-lauren-hawekotte-cfp--jymdc/

Here for you. (2024, June 4). National Domestic Violence Hotline. https://www.thehotline.org/

How to create a safe space at home for children. (2023, January 16). *Foster Plus.* https://www.fosterplus.co.uk/resources/news-blogs/blogs/how-to-create-a-safe-space-at-home-for-children/

How to make your parenting plan or agreement. (n.d.). Custody X Change. https://www.custodyxchange.com/topics/plans/overview/parenting-plan.php

How to prepare for a family court hearing: 10 tips. (2024, February 2). *O'Connor Family Law.* https://www.familylawma.com/blog/how-to-prepare-for-a-family-court-hearing-10-tips/

How to prepare for child custody court. (n.d.). Custody X Change. https://www.custodyxchange.com/topics/custody/steps/court.php

How to prove parental alienation. (2020, September 2). OnRecord. https://www.myonrecord.com/how-to-guides/how-to-prove-parental-alienation/

How to stop guilt-tripping: 10 steps for healthier interactions. (2024, July 5). *Calm Blog.* https://www.calm.com/blog/how-to-stop-guilt-tripping#

The importance of extended family. (n.d.). Family Law Nova Scotia. https://www.nsfamilylaw.ca/children/importance-extended-family

International organizations domestic violence national/global resources. (2014). DomesticShelters.org. https://www.domesticshelters.org/resources/national-global-organizations/international-organizations

Iriks, L. (2024, January 31). *Mindful co-parenting: The role of self-care and emotional intelligence.* The Co-Parenting Institute. https://thecoparentinginstitute.com.au/self-care-and-emotional-intelligence/

Jantz, G. (2023, March 7). *What are the five types of narcissism and how do they affect different types of relationships.* The Center, a Place of Hope. https://www.aplaceofhope.com/what-are-the-five-types-of-narcissism-and-how-do-they-affect-different-types-of-relationships/#

Joint legal custody defined. (n.d.). Custody X Change. https://www.custodyxchange.com/topics/custody/types/joint-legal-custody.php

Kemp, G., Smith, M., & Segal, J. (2024, February 5). *Children and divorce.* HelpGuide.org. https://www.helpguide.org/articles/parenting-family/children-and-divorce.htm

Kennedy, M. (2023, February 10). *How to hold your ground and get your point across when you're arguing with a narcissist.* Business Insider. https://www.businessinsider.com/guides/health/mental-health/how-to-argue-with-a-narcissist

Lawler, M. (2022, August 26). *How to start a self-care routine you'll follow.* Everyday Health. https://www.everydayhealth.com/self-care/start-a-self-care-routine/

Lebow, H. I. (2022, September 8). *Instilling and respecting co-parenting boundaries.* PsychCentral. https://psychcentral.com/relationships/co-parenting-boundaries

Lee, K. (2022, December 5). *How to nurture your parent-child bond.* Verywell Family. https://www.verywellfamily.com/habits-that-will-strengthen-your-parent-child-bond-620063

Leonard, J. (2023, August 23). *Am I narcissistic? How to tell.* Medical News Today. https://www.medicalnewstoday.com/articles/am-i-narcissistic

Lewis, K. (n.d.). *Parental alienation can be emotional child abuse.* https://www.ncsc.org/__data/assets/pdf_file/0014/42152/parental_alienation_Lewis.pdf

Lonczak, H. S. (2019, May 8). *What is positive parenting? 33 examples and benefits.* PositivePsychology.com. https://positivepsychology.com/positive-parenting/#benefits

Lundberg, A. (2024, February 27). *The long-term effects of narcissistic abuse.* Charlie Health. https://www.charliehealth.com/post/the-long-term-effects-of-narcissistic-abuse

Makin, S. (2023, January 2). *5 important conflict resolution steps: Your guide on conflict resolution.* Makin Wellness. https://www.makinwellness.com/conflict-resolution-steps/

Mandriota, M. (2022, March 11). *10 ways to talk to someone with narcissistic tendencies.* PsychCentral. https://psychcentral.com/disorders/how-to-talk-to-someone-with-narcissistic-tendencies#talking-to-a-narcissist

Marcin, A. (2020, March 20). *Co-parenting with a narcissist: Tips for making it work.* Healthline. https://www.healthline.com/health/parenting/co-parenting-with-a-narcissist

Marriage.com Editorial Team. (2024, May 9). *13 ways to get closure with a narcissist and move on.* Marriage.com.

https://www.marriage.com/advice/mental-health/getting-closure-with-narcissist

Martin, S. (2020, April 23). *7 types of boundaries you may need. PsychCentral.* https://psychcentral.com/blog/imperfect/2020/04/7-types-of-boundaries-you-may-need#Read-more-about-setting-boundaries

McGrath, L. (2021, May 10). *3 things grief taught me about resilience.* The House of Wellness. https://www.houseofwellness.com.au/wellbeing/mental-wellness/dr-lucy-hone-3-resilience-strategies

Merriam-Webster. (n.d.). Gaslighting. In *Merriam-Webster dictionary.* Retrieved July 13, 2024, from https://www.merriam-webster.com/dictionary/gaslighting

MFL Team. (2023, December 12). *From toddlers to teens: Navigating the co-parenting journey.* Modern Family Law. https://www.modernfamilylaw.com/resources/from-toddlers-to-teens-navigating-the-co-parenting-journey/

Mills, S. (2016). *Stress in children: Signs, symptoms and strategies.* Kids' Minds Matter. https://kidsmindsmatter.com/stress-in-children-signs-symptoms-and-strategies/

Moore, C. (2019, June 2). *How to practice self-compassion: 8 techniques and tips.* PositivePsychology.com. https://positivepsychology.com/how-to-practice-self-compassion/#8-tips-and-techniques-for-practicing-self-compassion

Narcissism. (n.d.). Psychology Today. https://www.psychologytoday.com/us/basics/narcissism

Narcissistic personality disorder. (2023, August 3). Cleveland Clinic. https://my.clevelandclinic.org/health/diseases/9742-narcissistic-personality-disorder

Nash, J. (2018, January 5). *How to set healthy boundaries & build positive relationships.* PositivePsychology.com. https://positivepsychology.com/great-self-care-setting-healthy-boundaries/#healthy

Navigating the journey of healing after divorce. (2023, December 22). *Thrive Psychology Group.* https://www.mythrivepsychology.com/thrive-blog/healing-after-divorce

9 steps to more effective parenting. (n.d.). Nemours Kids Health. https://kidshealth.org/en/parents/nine-steps.html

O'Bryan, A. (2022, February 8). *How to practice active listening: 16 examples & techniques.* PositivePsychology.com. https://positivepsychology.com/active-listening-techniques/

Obel, M. (2023, July 28). *Financial planning before, during, and after a divorce.* SmartAsset. https://smartasset.com/financial-advisor/divorce-financial-planning

Parental rights & parental responsibilities: Know yours. (2024). Custody X Change. https://www.custodyxchange.com/topics/custody/legal-concepts/parental-rights-responsibility.php

Parenting plan template. (2023, September 22). Legal Templates. https://legaltemplates.net/form/parenting-plan/

Patek, A. (2022, June 16). 10 ways to get your kids talking about their feelings. *Generation Mindful.* https://genmindful.com/blogs/mindful-moments/10-ways-to-get-your-kids-talking-about-their-feelings

Perry, E. (2022, April 13). How building healthy boundaries is the key to work relationships. *BetterUp*. https://www.betterup.com/blog/healthy-boundaries-in-relationships

Peterson, M. J. (2021). *Successful co-parenting: Third-party communication tips*. CentHQ. https://www.centhq.com/guides/topics/relationships/parenting/third-party-communication-parenting

Pharkin, K. L. (2021, July 26). Co-parenting with a narcissist: The impossible dream. *Psychology Today*. https://www.psychologytoday.com/za/blog/love-in-the-age-narcissism/202107/co-parenting-narcissist-the-impossible-dream

Protecting your mental health: Tips for co-parents. (2023, April 4). *Talking Parents*. https://talkingparents.com/blog/protecting-your-mental-health

Raypole, C. (2024a, January 29). *30 grounding techniques to quiet distressing thoughts*. Healthline. https://www.healthline.com/health/grounding-techniques

Raypole, C. (2024b, February 5). *10 signs of covert narcissism*. Healthline. https://www.healthline.com/health/covert-narcissist

Recovering from narcissistic abuse. (2016). I Believe You. https://www.ibelieveyourabuse.com/recovery

Resilience guide for parents and teachers. (2012, January 24). American Psychological Association. https://www.apa.org/topics/resilience/guide-parents-teachers

Resnick, A. (2023, November 9). *Dating after divorce: Knowing if you're ready and how to get started*. Verywell Mind.

https://www.verywellmind.com/how-to-start-dating-after-divorce-5191555

Robinson, C. (2024, March 20). *Successfully pivoting after a divorce: Career strategies.* Forbes. https://www.forbes.com/sites/cherylrobinson/2024/03/20/successfully-pivoting-after-a-divorce-career-strategies/

Routines: Positive behavior strategy. (2024, June 4). Raising Children Network. https://raisingchildren.net.au/preschoolers/behaviour/behaviour-management-tips-tools/routines

Rupp, K. (2018). Make co-parenting transitions easier—for you and your child. *OurFamilyWizard.* https://www.ourfamilywizard.com/blog/making-transitions-easier-children

Schneider, A. (2017, November 3). *Push-pull dynamic of a romantic relationship with a narcissist.* PsychCentral. https://psychcentral.com/blog/savvy-shrink/2017/11/push-pull-dynamic-of-a-romantic-relationship-with-a-narcissist#1

Scott, E. (2023, September 13). *18 effective stress relief strategies.* Verywell Mind. https://www.verywellmind.com/tips-to-reduce-stress-3145195

Segal, J., Kemp, G., & Smith, M. (2024, February 5). *Coping with a breakup or divorce.* HelpGuide.org. https://www.helpguide.org/articles/grief/dealing-with-a-breakup-or-divorce.htm

Segal, M. (2023, October 11). *The impact of co-parenting on relationships with extended family and friends.* Segal Law. https://www.marcysegal.com/the-impact-of-co-parenting-on-relationships-with-extended-family-and-friends/

Self-care for divorced parents: Prioritizing mental health and wellness. (2023, August 7). FLP: Ferguson Law Practice. https://fergusonlawpractice.com/self-care-for-divorced-parents-prioritizing-mental-health-and-wellness/

Self-talk. (2024, July 3). Healthdirect. https://www.healthdirect.gov.au/self-talk

Sember, B. (2023, November 22). 10 tips on how to reinvent yourself after divorce. *Divorce.com.* https://divorce.com/blog/finding-yourself-after-divorce/

Shafir, H. (2023, August 18). *Malignant narcissist: Traits, signs, causes, & how to deal with one.* Choosing Therapy. https://www.choosingtherapy.com/malignant-narcissist/

Shapiro, L. E. (2024, January 17). *How to prove parental alienation.* Shapiro Family Law. https://shapirofamilylaw.com/how-to-prove-parental-alienation/

6 financial planning steps in divorce. (2023, December 4). Burnett Attorneys & Notaries Inc. https://www.burnett-law.co.za/6-financial-planning-steps-in-divorce/

Skon, J. (2023, March 10). *Co-parenting advice: How to make the transition between households easier for parents and kids.* THE EXIT. https://theexit.com/co-parenting-advice-how-to-make-transition-between-households-easier-for-parents-kids

Soto, T. (2023, April 25). *The 4 stages of a narcissistic relationship pattern & how to end it.* mbgrelationships. https://www.mindbodygreen.com/articles/narcissistic-relationship-pattern

Spencer, E. (2023, April 13). *Healing—and finding love—after dating a narcissist.* Goop.

https://goop.com/wellness/relationships/dating-after-a-narcissistic-relationship/

Spotting the signs of emotional distress in children. (2019, April 29). *The Spark*. https://www.thespark.org.uk/blog/spotting-the-signs-of-emotional-distress-in-children-and-young-people/

Stewart, W. (2018, April 25). *10 steps for mindful conflict resolution*. Mindful. https://www.mindful.org/10-steps-for-mindful-conflict-resolution/

Stines, S. (2017, April 30). *Writing prompts for recovery from an abusive/toxic relationship*. PsychCentral. https://psychcentral.com/pro/recovery-expert/2017/04/writing-prompts-for-recovery-from-an-abusivetoxic-relationship#1

Sutton, J. (2020, October 1). *Self-esteem for kids: 30+ counseling tools & activities*. PositivePsychology.com. https://positivepsychology.com/self-esteem-for-children/#ways-to-build

Tapp, F. (2023, September 1). *30 journal prompts for kids to aid self-discovery*. Parents. https://www.parents.com/kids/education/30-journal-prompts-for-kids-to-aid-self-discovery/

Termini, A. M. (2018, February 27). How do I establish discipline in two homes after separation or divorce? *The Cooperative Parenting Institute*. https://cooperativeparenting.com/blog/discipline-across-households/

Tips to build emotional resilience in kids. (2022, August 10). Think Digital Academy. https://www.thinkdigitalacademy.org/tips-to-build-emotional-resilience-in-kids/

Wagner, L., & Turnbull, E. (2023, March 9). *How to recognize the 17 signs of parental alienation.* Doolan Wagner Family Lawyers. https://www.familylawyersdw.com.au/how-to-recognise-the-17-signs-of-parental-alienation/

WebMD Editorial Contributors. (2022, December 29). *Signs of parental alienation.* WebMD. https://www.webmd.com/mental-health/signs-parental-alienation

Weir, K. (2023, April 21). *How to help kids understand and manage their emotions.* American Psychological Association. https://www.apa.org/topics/parenting/emotion-regulation

What are "parental rights and responsibilities?" Is it the same thing as custody? (2023, November 28). WomensLaw.org. https://www.womenslaw.org/laws/me/custody/basic-information/what-are-parental-rights-and-responsibilities-it-same-thing

What if I can't afford a lawyer? (2023, October 16). *TalkingParents.* https://talkingparents.com/blog/what-if-i-cant-afford-a-lawyer

What is a healthy level of expectation for your child? (2023, June 23). St Peter's Preparatory School. https://stpetersprep.co.uk/news/what-is-healthy-level-expectation-for-your-child/

What is love bombing, and what does it look like? (2023, August 18). Nebraska Medicine. https://www.nebraskamed.com/health/conditions-and-services/behavioral-health/what-is-love-bombing-and-what-does-it-look-like#

What is post-traumatic stress disorder (PTSD)? (2022, November). American Psychiatric Association. https://www.psychiatry.org/patients-families/ptsd/what-is-ptsd

What is the difference between co-parenting and parallel parenting? (2024, February 12). Men's & Fathers' Rights Divorce Lawyers. https://mensrightsdivorcelaw.com/co-parenting-and-parallel-parenting/

White, S. (2021, June 24). *How to set goals during a breakup or divorce.* Medium. https://medium.com/@sonyan_65563/how-to-set-goals-during-a-breakup-or-divorce-9c1364acd466

Woolrych, D. (2024, January 22). 10 tips to combat parental alienation (2024 update). *Lawpath.* https://lawpath.com.au/blog/10-tips-to-combat-parental-alienation

Young children and communication. (2012, July 31). Better Health Channel. https://www.betterhealth.vic.gov.au/health/healthyliving/young-children-and-communication

Zhu, J., Xiang, S., & Li, Y. (2024). Mothers' perceived co-parenting and preschooler's problem behaviors: The mediating role of maternal parenting stress and the moderating role of family resilience. *Psychology Research and Behavior Management, Volume 17*, 891–904. https://doi.org/10.2147/prbm.s451870

Zung, R. (2024). *Conflict to confidence: Creating financial independence after a narcissist* [Video]. YouTube. https://www.youtube.com/watch?v=8K_EKUmGJyA

Image References

Ali, A. (2018). *Blue ballpoint pen on paper beside calculator* [Image]. Unsplash. https://unsplash.com/photos/blue-ballpoint-pen-on-paper-beside-calculator-JLW-T4LiJCw

Anton, A. (2016). *Photo of gel candle on board beside pillow* [Image]. Unsplash. https://unsplash.com/photos/photo-of-gel-candle-on-board-beside-pillow-u_z0X-yrJIE

Buscher, N. (2018). *The earth and I* [Image]. Unsplash. https://unsplash.com/photos/green-plant-x8ZStukS2PM

Busing, H. (2020). *Girl friends hands piled together* [Image]. Unsplash. https://unsplash.com/photos/person-in-red-sweater-holding-babys-hand-Zyx1bK9mqmA

Content Pixie. (2021). *A book sitting on top of a table next to a laptop* [Image]. Unsplash. https://unsplash.com/photos/a-book-sitting-on-top-of-a-table-next-to-a-laptop-iXRVqQtBa_8

Cottonbro Studio. (2020). *Man in black suit sitting on brown wooden chair* [Image]. Pexels. https://www.pexels.com/photo/man-in-black-suit-sitting-on-brown-wooden-chair-4098270/

Geralt. (2016). *Banner, header, attention* [Image]. Pixabay. https://pixabay.com/illustrations/banner-header-attention-caution-1165980/

Geralt. (2022). *Law, family, gavel* [Image]. Pixabay. https://pixabay.com/illustrations/law-family-gavel-mallet-justice-7157621/

Howard, M. (2017). *Mountain pass during sunrise* [Image]. Unsplash. https://unsplash.com/photos/mountain-pass-during-sunrise-A4iL43vunlY

Jopwell. (2019). *Woman wearing teal dress sitting on chair talking to man* [Image]. Pexels. https://www.pexels.com/photo/woman-wearing-teal-dress-sitting-on-chair-talking-to-man-2422280/

Kaboompics. (2015). *Organizer, calendar, schedule* [Image]. Pixabay. https://pixabay.com/photos/organizer-calendar-schedule-791939/

Kampus Production. (2021). *Father and daughter sitting on the floor* [Image]. Pexels. https://www.pexels.com/photo/father-and-daughter-sitting-on-the-floor-8949326/

Lusina, A. (2021). *Woman with long nails writing text in diary* [Image]. Pexels. https://www.pexels.com/photo/woman-with-long-nails-writing-text-in-diary-7256738/

National Cancer Institute. (2020). *Happy birthday to you greeting card* [Image]. Unsplash. https://unsplash.com/photos/happy-birthday-to-you-greeting-card-vbuR2q56EZM

No Revisions. (2018). *A person using a vacuum to clean a carpet* [Image]. Unsplash. https://unsplash.com/photos/a-person-using-a-vacuum-to-clean-a-carpet-cpIgNaazQ6w

Obymaha, D. (2018). *Mother and daughter on grass* [Image]. Pexels. https://www.pexels.com/photo/mother-and-daughter-on-grass-1683975/

Podrez, A. (2021). *Two children sitting inside the tent* [Image]. Pexels. https://www.pexels.com/photo/two-children-sitting-inside-the-tent-7494477/

Shkraba, A. (2020). *Photograph of a child reading a book with her father* [Image]. Pexels. https://www.pexels.com/photo/photograph-of-a-child-reading-a-book-with-her-father-5571735/

StockSnap. (2017). *Still items things* [Image]. Pixabay. https://pixabay.com/photos/still-items-things-book-notebook-2607441/

Wolff, C. (2018). *Person crying beside bed* [Image]. Unsplash. https://unsplash.com/photos/person-crying-beside-bed-owBcefxgrIE

Printed in Dunstable, United Kingdom